Günter Grass

In the Egg
and Other Poems

In German with translations by

Michael Hamburger and

Christopher Middleton

A Harvest Book

A Helen and Kurt Wolff Book

Harcourt Brace Jovanovich

New York and London

The following translations have appeared before: "Open Wardrobe," "The School for Tenors," "Prevention of Cruelty to Animals" and "Transformation" in *Modern German Poetry 1910–1960*, an Anthology with Verse Translations, edited and with an Introduction by Michael Hamburger and Christopher Middleton, published by Grove Press, Inc., copyright © 1962 by Michael Hamburger & Christopher Middleton; "Unsuccessful Raid" and "Family Matters" in *Evergreen Review*, Volume 9, Number 36, June 1965, copyright © 1965 by Evergreen Review, Inc.; "The Midge Plague," "Open Air Concert," "Sale," "Don't Turn Round," "New Mysticism," "Taking Breath," "Wrong Beauty" and "March" in *The Times Literary Supplement*; "Folding Chairs," "Happiness," "Normandy," "The Sea Battle," "Askesis" and "Chefs and Spoons" in *Encounter*; "Powerless, with a Guitar," "Do Something," "The Jellied Pig's Head" and "The Epilogue" in *New American Review, Number 2*.

Library of Congress Cataloging in Publication Data

Grass, Günter, date —
    In the egg and other poems.

    (A Harvest book ; 352)
    "A Helen and Kurt Wolff book."
    Consists of the author's Selected poems, and of his New poems, which was a selection from Ausgefragt.
    I. Title.
PT2613.R338A24   1977   831'.9'14   76-40441
ISBN 0-15-672239-9

First Harvest edition 1977

A B C D E F G H I J

The translations on pages 3, 7, 9, 17, 25,
43, 45, and 55 are by Christopher Middleton.
The rest, by Michael Hamburger.

Contents

NEW POEMS

SELECTED POEMS

An alle Gärtner

Warum wollt ihr mir verbieten Fleisch zu essen?
Jetzt kommt ihr mit Blumen,
bereitet mir Astern zu,
als bliebe vom Herbst nicht Nachgeschmack genug.
Laßt die Nelken im Garten.
Sind die Mandeln doch bitter,
der Gasometer,
den ihr den Kuchen nennt—
und ihr schneidet mir ab,
bis ich nach Milch verlange.
Ihr sagt: Gemüse,—
und verkauft mir Rosen im Kilo.
Gesund, sagt ihr und meint die Tulpen.
Soll ich das Gift,
zu kleinen Sträußchen gebunden,
mit etwas Salz verspeisen?
Soll ich an Maiglöckchen sterben?
Und die Lilien auf meinem Grab,—
wer wird mich vor den Vegetariern schützen?

Laßt mich vom Fleisch essen.
Laßt mich mit dem Knochen alleine,
damit er die Scham verliert und sich nackt zeigt.
Erst wenn ich vom Teller rücke
und den Ochsen laut ehre,
dann erst öffnet die Gärten,
damit ich Blumen kaufen kann—
weil ich sie gerne welken sehe.

To All Gardeners

Why should you tell me to eat no meat?
Now you come to me with flowers,
prepare asters,
as if autumn's aftertaste was not enough.
Leave the carnations in the garden.
So what, the almonds are bitter,
the gasometer
which you call the cake—
and you cut me a piece
till I ask for milk.
You say: vegetables—
and sell me roses by the kilo.
Healthy, you say, and mean the tulips.
Should I eat with some salt
the poison
tied in little bunches?
Should I die of lilies-of-the-valley?
And the lilies on my grave—
who'll protect me from the vegetarians?

Let me eat meat.
Let me be, with the bone.
Let the bone lose all shame and show itself naked.
Only when I rise from the plate
and loudly do the ox honour,
only then open up the gardens
for me to buy flowers—
because I like to see them dying.

Geöffneter Schrank

Unten stehen die Schuhe.
Sie fürchten sich vor einem Käfer
auf dem Hinweg,
vor einem Pfennig auf dem Rückweg,
vor Käfer und Pfennig die sie treten könnten
bis es sich einprägt.
Oben ist die Heimat der Hüte.
Behüte, hüte dich, behutsam.
Unglaubliche Federn,
wie hieß der Vogel,
wohin rollte sein Blick
als er einsah, daß er zu bunt geraten?
Die weißen Kugeln, die in den Taschen schlafen,
träumen von Motten.
Hier fehlt ein Knopf,
im Gürtel ermüdet die Schlange.
Schmerzliche Seide,
Astern und andere feuergefährliche Blumen,
der Herbst, der zum Kleid wird,
jeden Sonntag mit Fleisch und dem Salz
gefälteter Wäsche gefüllt.
Bevor der Schrank schweigt, Holz wird,
ein entfernter Verwandter der Kiefer,—
wer wird den Mantel tragen
wenn du einmal tot bist?
Seinen Arm im Ärmel bewegen,
zuvorkommend jeder Bewegung?
Wer wird den Kragen hochschlagen,
vor den Bildern stehen bleiben
und alleine sein unter der windigen Glocke?

Open Wardrobe

The shoes are at the bottom.
They are afraid of a beetle
on the way out,
of a penny on the way back,
of a beetle and a penny on which they might tread
till it impresses itself.
At the top is the home of the headgear.
Take heed, be wary, not headstrong.
Incredible feathers,
what was the bird called,
where did its eyes roll
when it knew that its wings were too gaudy?
The white balls asleep in the pockets
dream of moths.
Here a button is missing,
in this belt the snake grows weary.
Doleful silk,
asters and other inflammable flowers,
autumn becoming a dress.
Every Sunday filled with flesh
and the salt of creased linen.
Before the wardrobe falls silent, turns into wood,
a distant relation of pine-trees—
who will wear the coat
one day when you're dead?
Who move his arm in the sleeve,
anticipate every movement?
Who will turn up the collar,
stop in front of the pictures
and be alone under the windy cloche?

Hochwasser

Wir warten den Regen ab,
obgleich wir uns daran gewöhnt haben
hinter der Gardine zu stehen, unsichtbar zu sein.
Löffel ist Sieb geworden, niemand wagt mehr
die Hand auszustrecken.
Es schwimmt jetzt Vieles in den Straßen
das man während der trockenen Zeit sorgfältig verbarg.
Wie peinlich des Nachbarn verbrauchte Betten zu sehen.
Oft stehen wir vor dem Pegel
und vergleichen unsere Besorgnis wie Uhren.
Manches läßt sich regulieren.
Doch wenn die Behälter überlaufen, das ererbte Maß voll ist,
werden wir beten müssen.
Der Keller steht unter Wasser, wir haben die Kisten hochgetragen
und prüfen den Inhalt mit der Liste.
Noch ist nichts verloren gegangen.—
Weil das Wasser jetzt sicher bald fällt
haben wir begonnen Sonnenschirmchen zu nähen.
Es wird sehr schwer sein wieder über den Platz zu gehen,
deutlich, mit bleischwerem Schatten.
Wir werden den Vorhang am Anfang vermissen
und oft in den Keller steigen
um den Strich zu betrachten,
den das Wasser uns hinterließ.

The Flood

We are waiting for the rain to stop,
although we have got accustomed
to standing behind the curtain, being invisible.
Spoons have become sieves, nobody dares now
to stretch a hand out.
Many things are floating in the streets,
things people carefully hid in the dry time.
How awkward to see your neighbour's stale old beds.
Often we stand by the water-gauge
and compare our worries like watches.
Some things can be regulated.
But when the butts overflow, the inherited cup fills,
we shall have to pray.
The cellar is submerged, we brought the crates up
and are checking their contents against the list.
So far nothing has been lost.—
Because the water is now certain to drop soon,
we have begun to sew sunshades.
It will be difficult to cross the square once more,
distinct, with a shadow heavy as lead.
We shall miss the curtain at first,
and go into the cellar often
to consider the mark
which the water bequeathed us.

Die Mückenplage

In unserem Bezirk wird es von Jahr zu Jahr schlimmer.
Oft laden wir Besuch um den Schwarm etwas zu teilen.
Doch die Leute gehen bald wieder,—
nachdem sie den Käse gelobt haben.

Es ist nicht der Stich.
Nein, das Gefühl, daß etwas geschieht,
das älter ist als die Hand—
und im Besitz jeder Zukunft.

Wenn die Betten still sind
und der schwarze Stein an unzähligen, tönenden Fäden hängt,
Fäden die reißen und wieder neu,
etwas heller beginnen,

wenn ich eine Pfeife anbrenne
und nach dem See hin sitze,
auf dem ein dichtes Geräusch schwimmt,
bin ich hilflos.

Wir wollen jetzt nicht mehr schlafen.
Meine Söhne sind hellwach,
die Töchter drängen vor dem Spiegel,
meine Frau hat Kerzen gestellt.

Nun glauben wir an Flammen,
die zwanzig Pfennige kosten,
denen die Mücken sich nähern,
einer kurzen Verheißung.

The Midge Plague

It's getting worse hereabouts every year.
Often we have guests in, to share the swarm.
But soon people leave again—
having commended the cheese.

It's not the sting.
No, but the sense that what's going on
is older than the hand—
and has every future in its grasp.

When the beds go quiet
and the black stone hangs by innumerable singing threads,
threads which break and start again,
mended, a little more clear,

when I light a pipe
and sit facing the lake
with a thick sound swimming over it,
I'm helpless.

Let's give up trying to sleep.
My sons are wide awake,
my daughters crowd to the mirror,
my wife has lit candles.

Now we pin our faith on flames
costing twenty pfennigs,
which the midges come to,
a brief promise.

Die Schule der Tenöre

Nimm den Lappen, wische den Mond fort,
schreibe die Sonne, die andere Münze
über den Himmel, die Schultafel.
Setze dich dann.
Dein Zeugnis wird gut sein,
du wirst versetzt werden,
eine neue, hellere Mütze tragen.
Denn die Kreide hat recht
und der Tenor der sie singt.
Er wird den Samt entblättern,
Efeu, Meterware der Nacht,
Moos, ihren Unterton,
jede Amsel wird er vertreiben.

Den Bassisten, mauert ihn ein
in seinem Gewölbe.
Wer glaubt noch an Fässer
in denen der Wein fällt?
Ob Vogel oder Schrapnell,
oder nur Summen bis es knackt,
weil der Äther überfüllt ist
mit Wochenend und Sommerfrische.
Scheren, die in den Schneiderstuben
das Lied von Frühling und Konfektion zwitschern,—
hieran kein Beispiel.

Die Brust heraus, bis der Wind seinen Umweg macht.
Immer wieder Trompeten,
spitzgedrehte Tüten voller silberner Zwiebeln.
Dann die Geduld.
Warten, bis der Dame die Augen davonlaufen,
zwei unzufriedene Dienstmädchen.
Jetzt erst den Ton den die Gläser fürchten
und der Staub
der die Gesimse verfolgt bis sie hinken.

The School for Tenors

Take your duster, wipe away the moon,
write the sun, that other coin
across the sky, the blackboard.
Then take your seat.
Your report will be a good one,
You will go up one class,
wear a new, a brighter cap.
For the chalk is in the right
and so is the tenor who sings it.
He will unroll the velvet,
ivy, yard-measured wares of night,
moss, its undertone,
every blackbird he'll drive away.

The bass—immure him
in his vault.
Who now believes in barrels
in which the wine-level falls?
Whether bird or shrapnel
or only a hum till it cracks
because the ether is overcrowded
with weekend and sea-side resort.
Scissors which in the tailors' workshops
twitter the song of springtime and haute couture—
this no example.

Puff out your chest, till the wind takes its devious way.
Trumpets again and again,
conical paper bags full of silver onions.
After that, patience.
Wait till the lady's eyes run away,
two dissatisfied skivvies.
Only now that tone which the glasses fear
and the dust
that pursues the ledges until they limp.

Fischgräten, wer singt diese Zwischenräume,
den Mittag, mit Schilf gespießt?
Wie schön sang Else Fenske, als sie,
während der Sommerferien,
in großer Höhe daneben trat,
in einen stillen Gletscherspalt stürzte,
uns nur ihr Schirmchen
und das hohe C zurückließ.

Das hohe C, die vielen Nebenflüsse des Mississippi,
der herrliche Atem,
der die Kuppeln erfand und den Beifall.
Vorhang, Vorhang, Vorhang.
Schnell, bevor der Leuchter nicht mehr klirren will,
bevor die Galerien knicken
und die Seide billig wird.
Vorhang, bevor du den Beifall begreifst.

Fishbones, who will sing these gaps,
sing noon impaled with rushes?
How well did Elsie Fenner sing
when, in the summer vacation
at a great height she took a false step,
tumbled into a silent glacier crevasse
and left nothing behind but
her little parasol and the high C.

The high C, the many tributaries of the Mississippi,
the glorious breath
that invented cupolas and applause.
Curtain, curtain, curtain.
Quick before the candelabrum refuses to jingle,
before the galleries droop
and silk becomes cheap.
Curtain, before you understand the applause.

Musik im Freien

Als die Pause überwunden schien
kam Aurele mit dem Knochen.
Seht meine Flöte und mein weißes Hemd,
seht die Giraffe die über den Zaun späht,
das ist mein Blut, welches zuhört.
Nun will ich alle Drosseln besiegen.

Als der gelbe Hund über die Wiese lief
verendete das Konzert.
Später fand man den Knochen nicht mehr.
Die Noten lagen unter den Stühlen,
der Kapellmeister nahm sein Luftgewehr
und erschoß alle Amseln.

Open Air Concert

When the interval seemed to have been overcome
Aurelia arrived with the bone.
Look at my flute and my white shift,
look at the giraffe peering over the fence,
those are my blood, which is listening.
Now I'll defeat all the thrushes.

When the yellow dog ran over the meadow
the concert expired.
Later the bone could not be found.
The scores lay under the chairs,
the conductor seized his air-gun
and shot all the blackbirds.

Die Klingel

Versuche mit Tinte,
Niederschriften im Rauch,
halb erwacht
im Dickicht süßer Gardinen.
Die Straße, den Notverband wieder aufgerollt
weil die Wunde juckt,
weil die Erinnerung sich stückeln läßt und längen
so eine Katze unterm Streicheln.

Wer bewegte die Klingel,
belud die Luft mit Erfolg.
War es das Glück,
mit neuen, dünneren Strümpfen
oder der Mann
mit dem Krankenschein unter der Haut.
Niemand erschrak. Nicht das Wasser zum Spülen,
kleinen Frauen im Zimmer kräuselte sauer der Rock.

Wer kann eine Klingel wieder verkaufen,
zurücktreten, mit dem Hut in der Hand,
die Kreide der Herkunft vom Zaun lecken.
Die nackte Gestalt wird zwischen den Spiegeln
keinen Vorsprung gewinnen.
Keine Bewegung kommt hier zu kurz.
Gleichzeitig wird es hüsteln,
das Weiße im Auge vergilben,
der falsche Bart,
ein letztes Geständnis,
von der Oberlippe wird sich der Rauch lösen
und keinen Vogel begeistern.

The Doorbell

Essays with ink,
inscribings in the smoke,
half wakened
in the thicket of sweet curtains.
The street, the bandage rolled up again,
because the wound is twitching,
because memory can be assembled and stretched—
some cat being stroked.

Who pushed the bell,
loaded the air with success.
Was it happiness
with new, sheerer stockings,
or the man
with the medical card under his skin.
No one jumped. Not the dish water,
sourly the skirts of little women crinkled in the room.

Who can sell back a doorbell,
withdraw, hat in hand,
lick from the fence his origin's chalk-mark.
The naked figure will not get ahead
between the mirrors.
Here no motion falls too short.
There'll be a slight simultaneous coughing,
the whites of eyes yellowing,
the false beard,
a last admission,
smoke shall be loosed from the upper lip
and excite no bird.

Der elfte Finger

Wo blieb mein elfter Finger,
mein elfter, besonderer Finger,
niemals hat er gelacht,
niemals den Handschuh, die Nacht
wegen der Farbe getragen.
Er hat die Ziege gemelkt.
Er hat die Ziege gemelkt,
hat die Ziege der Uhr zugetrieben,
die Ziege hat sich gebückt.
Konnte sich bücken, konnte der Uhr,
hat der Uhr die Sohlen geleckt,
bis die Uhr kicherte, kicherte,
alle Minuten verlor,
alles, auch ihre Pausen gestand.
Nun sah er im Weiten schon Gold,
der Finger sah weither schon Gold,
hat Juweliere verführt,
Bräute, kurz vor der Kirche.
Schlüssel war er, Stempel, Verschweigen,—
oft habe ich meinen elften Finger geschleckt,
obgleich er niemals schlief,
obgleich er niemals schlief.

Worauf soll ich nun deuten?
Worauf soll ich nun deuten,
heute, da beide verkürzten Hände
nur noch geschickt sind
Eisen wie Fleisch, Fleisch, einen Amboß zu tasten,—
oder sie hocken am Abend gleich belasteten Krähen
auf einem Stein im Feld,
zählen acht, neun, zehn, niemals elf.
Niemals zählen sie elf.

The Eleventh Finger

Where is my eleventh finger,
my eleventh, my special finger,
not once has it laughed,
not once worn the glove, the night
because of their colour.
It milked the goat.
It milked the goat,
and drove the goat to the clock;
the goat bent down.
Was able to bend, could lick,
did lick the soles of the clock
till the clock tittering, tittering,
lost all its minutes, made
a clean breast of everything, even the stops.
Now far off it saw gold,
the finger saw gold from afar,
a seducer of jewellers, brides
on the very threshold of churches.
A key it was, a stamp, a silence—
often I've sucked my eleventh finger
although it never slept,
although it never slept.

At what am I now to point?
At what am I now to point,
today, when both my shortened hands
are good for nothing but
to feel flesh like iron, flesh, and an anvil—
or evenings they crouch like dejected crows
on a stone in a field,
counting eight, nine, ten, never eleven—
they never count eleven.

Tierschutz

Das Klavier in den Zoo.
Schnell, bringt das Zebra in die gute Stube.
Seid freundlich mit ihm,
es kommt aus Bechstein.
Noten frißt es
und unsere süßen Ohren.

Nächtliches Stadion

Langsam ging der Fußball am Himmel auf.
Nun sah man, daß die Tribüne besetzt war.
Einsam stand der Dichter im Tor,
doch der Schiedsrichter pfiff: Abseits.

Misslungener Überfall

Am Mittwoch.
Jeder wußte wieviele Treppen hinauf,
den Druck auf den Knopf,
die zweite Tür links.
Sie stürmten die Kasse.
Es war aber Sonntag
und das Geld in der Kirche.

Familiär

In unserem Museum,—wir besuchen es jeden Sonntag,—
hat man eine neue Abteilung eröffnet.
Unsere abgetriebenen Kinder, blasse, ernsthafte Embryos,
sitzen dort in schlichten Gläsern
und sorgen sich um die Zukunft ihrer Eltern.

Prevention of Cruelty to Animals

The piano into the zoo.
Quick, get the zebra into the best room.
Be kind to it,
it comes from Bechstein.
Scores are its fodder,
and our sweet ears.

Stadium at Night

Slowly the football rose in the sky.
Now one could see that the stands were packed.
Alone the poet stood at the goal
but the referee whistled: Off-side.

Unsuccessful Raid

On Wednesday.
Everyone knew how many steps,
which bell to ring,
the second door on the left.
They smashed the till.
But it was Sunday
and the cash was at church.

Family Matters

In our museum—we always go there on Sundays—
they have opened a new department.
Our aborted children, pale, serious embryos,
sit there in plain glass jars
and worry about their parents' future.

Möbel im Freien

Wer warf die Gartenbank um?
Nun liegt sie da, grün und vergeblich,
stottert mit vier bewiesenen Beinen,
sucht den Beweis in der Luft.
Aufstellen wieder. Wieder wie vorher
unter dem Sommer sitzen und Kaffee
mit einer Tante trinken und Kekse,
Hostien brechen.

Nein, dieser Sommer ist pleite.
Die Tante nährt weiße Würmer,
die Kekse krümeln und passen
in keine ererbte Monstranz.
Auch trinkst du den Kaffee
zu heiß, halb im Weggehn,
flüchtig, mit sichernden Blicken
nach links, nach rechts und nach links.

Gartenbänke die einmal gestürzt,
stehen nun ledig, kundig des Herbstes,
zwischen den nassen Stachelbeersträuchern,
vom Regen, Aufbruch, mitten im Satz,
vom Mond der nie stillsitzt bevölkert.

Furniture out of Doors

Who up-ended the garden seat?
Now here it lies, useless and green,
stammers with four proven legs,
looks for the proof in the air.
Stand it up again. As before
to sit beneath the summer,
drink tea with an aunt and break
biscuits, holy wafers.

No, this summer is done for.
The aunt is feeding white worms,
the biscuits are crumbling and fit
into no inherited pyx.
Also, you're drinking your tea
too hot, on the point of leaving,
rushed, with defensive glances
to the left, to the right, to the left.

Once up-ended, garden seats
stand vacant, conscious of autumn,
between wet gooseberry bushes,
occupied only by rain, departure, the sentence cut short,
by the moon that never sits still.

Blechmusik

Damals schliefen wir in einer Trompete.
Es war sehr still dort,
wir träumten von keinem Signal,
lagen, wie zum Beweis,
mit offenem Mund in der Schlucht,—
damals, ehe wir ausgestoßen.

War es ein Kind, auf dem Kopf
einen Helm aus gelesener Zeitung,
war es ein irrer Husar
der auf Befehl aus dem Bild trat,
war es schon damals der Tod,
der so seinen Stempel behauchte?

Heute, ich weiß nicht wer uns geweckt hat,
vermummt als Blumen in Vasen
oder in Zuckerdosen,
von jedem bedroht der Kaffee trinkt
und sein Gewissen befragt:
Ein oder zwei Stückchen oder gar drei.

Nun fliehen wir und mit uns unser Gepäck.
Alle halbleeren Tüten, jeden Trichter im Bier,
kaum verlassene Mäntel, stehengebliebene Uhren,
Gräber die andre bezahlten
und Frauen die sehr wenig Zeit haben,
füllen wir kurzfristig aus.

In Schubladen voller Wäsche und Liebe,
in einem Ofen der Nein sagt
und nur seinen Standpunkt erwärmt,
in einem Telefon blieben unsere Ohren zurück
und hören, nun schon versöhnlich,
dem neuen Zeichen Besetzt zu.

Music for Brass

Those days we slept in a trumpet.
It was very quiet in there,
we never dreamed it would sound,
lay, as if to prove it,
open-mouthed in the gorge—
those days, before we were blown out.

Was it a child, on his head
a helmet of studied newspaper,
was it a scatty hussar
who walked at a command out of the picture,
was it even those days death
who breathed that way on his rubber stamp?

Today, I don't know who woke us,
disguised as flowers in vases,
or else in sugar bowls,
threatened by anyone who drinks coffee
and questions his conscience:
one lump or two, or even three.

Now we're on the run and our luggage with us.
All half-empty paper bags, every crater in our beer,
cast-off coats, clocks that have stopped,
graves paid for by other people,
and women very short of time,
for a while we fill them.

In drawers full of linen and love,
in a stove which says no
and warms its own standpoint only,
in a telephone our ears have stayed behind
and listen, already conciliant,
to the new tone for busy.

Damals schliefen wir in einer Trompete.
Hin und zurück träumten wir,
Alleen gleichmäßig bepflanzt.
Auf ruhigem, endlosem Rücken
lagen wir jenem Gewölbe an
und träumten von keinem Signal.

Those days we slept in a trumpet.
Backward and forward we dreamed,
avenues, symmetrically planted.
On a tranquil unending back
we lay against that arch,
and never dreamed it would sound.

Wandlung

Plötzlich waren die Kirschen da,
obgleich ich vergessen hatte,
daß es Kirschen gibt
und verkünden ließ: Noch nie gab es Kirschen—
waren sie da, plötzlich und teuer.

Pflaumen fielen und trafen mich.
Doch wer da denkt,
ich wandelte mich,
weil etwas fiel und mich traf,
wurde noch nie von fallenden Pflaumen getroffen.

Erst als man Nüsse in meine Schuhe schüttete
und ich laufen mußte,
weil die Kinder die Kerne wollten,
schrie ich nach Kirschen, wollt ich von Pflaumen
getroffen werden—und wandelte mich ein wenig.

Transformation

Suddenly the cherries were there
although I had forgotten
that cherries exist
and caused to be proclaimed: There never have been cherries—
they were there, suddenly and dear.

Plums fell and hit me;
but whoever thinks
that I was transformed
because something fell and hit me
has never been hit by falling plums.

Only when they poured nuts into my shoes
and I had to walk
because the children wanted the kernels
I cried out for cherries, wanted plums
to hit me—and was transformed a little.

Klappstühle

Wie traurig sind diese Veränderungen.
Die Leute schrauben ihre Namenschilder ab,
nehmen den Topf mit dem Rotkohl,
wärmen ihn auf, anderen Ortes.

Was sind das für Möbel,
die für den Aufbruch werben?
Die Leute nehmen ihre Klappstühle
und wandern aus.

Mit Heimweh und Brechreiz beladene Schiffe
tragen patentierte Sitzgelegenheiten
und patentlose Besitzer
hin und her.

Auf beiden Seiten des großen Wassers
stehen nun Klappstühle;
wie traurig sind diese Veränderungen.

Folding Chairs

How sad these changes are.
People unscrew the nameplates from the doors,
take the saucepan of cabbage
and heat it up again, in a different place.

What sort of furniture is this
that advertises departure?
People take up their folding chairs
and emigrate.

Ships laden with homesickness and the urge to vomit
carry patented seating contraptions
and their unpatented owners
to and fro.

Now on both sides of the great ocean
there are folding chairs;
how sad these changes are.

Kirschen

Wenn die Liebe auf Stelzen
über die Kieswege stochert
und in die Bäume reicht,
möchte auch ich gerne Kirschen
in Kirschen als Kirschen erkennen,

nicht mehr mit Armen zu kurz,
mit Leitern, denen es immer
an einer Sprosse mangelt,
von Fallobst leben, Kompott.

Süß und süßer, fast schwarz;
Amseln träumen so rot—
wer küßt hier wen,
wenn die Liebe
auf Stelzen in Bäume reicht.

Cherries

When love on stilts
picks its way along gravel paths
and reaches the treetops
I too in cherries would like
to experience cherries as cherries,

no longer with arms too short,
with ladders on which for ever
one rung, just one rung is missing,
to live on stewed fruit, on windfalls.

Sweet and sweeter, darkening;
a red such as blackbirds dream—
who here is kissing whom,
when love
reaches the treetops on stilts.

Stapellauf

Wenn es die Möwe verlangt,
werde ich ein Schiff bauen,
werde beim Stapellauf
glücklich sein,
ein blendendes Hemd tragen,
vielleicht auch Sekt weinen
oder Schmierseife absondern,
ohne die es nicht geht.

Wer wird die Rede halten?
Wer kann vom Blatt lesen
ohne zu erblinden?
Der Präsident?
Auf welchen Namen soll ich dich taufen?
Soll ich deinen Untergang ANNA nennen
oder COLUMBUS?

Launching

If the seagull insists
I shall build a ship,
shall be happy at
the launching,
wear a dazzling shirt,
perhaps also weep champagne
or secrete soft soap,
both being indispensable.

Who will make the speech?
Who can sight-read the words
without going blind?
The President?
By what name shall I christen you?
Shall I call your sinking ANNA
or else COLUMBUS?

Im Ei

Wir leben im Ei.
Die Innenseite der Schale
haben wir mit unanständigen Zeichnungen
und den Vornamen unserer Feinde bekritzelt.
Wir werden gebrütet.

Wer uns auch brütet,
unseren Bleistift brütet er mit.
Ausgeschlüpft eines Tages,
werden wir uns sofort
ein Bildnis des Brütenden machen.

Wir nehmen an, daß wir gebrütet werden.
Wir stellen uns ein gutmütiges Geflügel vor
und schreiben Schulaufsätze
über Farbe und Rasse
der uns brütenden Henne.

Wann schlüpfen wir aus?
Unsere Propheten im Ei
streiten sich für mittelmäßige Bezahlung
über die Dauer der Brutzeit.
Sie nehmen einen Tag X an.

Aus Langeweile und echtem Bedürfnis
haben wir Brutkästen erfunden.
Wir sorgen uns sehr um unseren Nachwuchs im Ei.
Gerne würden wir jener, die über uns wacht
unser Patent empfehlen.

Wir aber haben ein Dach überm Kopf.
Senile Küken,
Embryos mit Sprachkenntnissen
reden den ganzen Tag
und besprechen noch ihre Träume.

In the Egg

We live in the egg.
We have covered the inside wall
of the shell with dirty drawings
and the Christian names of our enemies.
We are being hatched.

Whoever is hatching us
is hatching our pencils as well.
Set free from the egg one day
at once we shall make an image
of whoever is hatching us.

We assume that we're being hatched.
We imagine some good-natured fowl
and write school essays
about the colour and breed
of the hen that is hatching us.

When shall we break the shell?
Our prophets inside the egg
for a middling salary argue
about the period of incubation.
They posit a day called X.

Out of boredom and genuine need
we have invented incubators.
We are much concerned about our offspring inside the egg.
We should be glad to recommend our patent
to her who looks after us.

But we have a roof over our heads.
Senile chicks,
polyglot embryos
chatter all day
and even discuss their dreams.

Und wenn wir nun nicht gebrütet werden?
Wenn diese Schale niemals ein Loch bekommt?
Wenn unser Horizont nur der Horizont
unserer Kritzeleien ist und auch bleiben wird?
Wir hoffen, daß wir gebrütet werden.

Wenn wir auch nur noch vom Brüten reden,
bleibt doch zu befürchten, daß jemand,
außerhalb unserer Schale, Hunger verspürt,
uns in die Pfanne haut und mit Salz bestreut.—
Was machen wir dann, ihr Brüder im Ei?

And what if we're not being hatched?
If this shell will never break?
If our horizon is only that
of our scribbles, and always will be?
We hope that we're being hatched.

Even if we only talk of hatching
there remains the fear that someone
outside our shell will feel hungry
and crack us into the frying pan with a pinch of salt.
What shall we do then, my brethren inside the egg?

Glück

Ein leerer Autobus
stürzt durch die ausgesternte Nacht.
Vielleicht singt sein Chauffeur
und ist glücklich dabei.

Normandie

Die Bunker am Strand
können ihren Beton nicht loswerden.
Manchmal kommt ein halbtoter General
und streichelt Schießscharten.
Oder es wohnen Touristen
für fünf verquälte Minuten—
Wind, Sand, Papier und Urin:
Immer ist Invasion.

Die Seeschlacht

Ein amerikanischer Flugzeugträger
und eine gotische Kathedrale
versenkten sich
mitten im Stillen Ozean
gegenseitig.
Bis zum Schluß
spielte der junge Vikar auf der Orgel.—
Nun hängen Flugzeuge und Engel in der Luft
und können nicht landen.

Happiness

An empty bus
hurtles through the starry night.
Perhaps the driver is singing
and is happy because he sings.

Normandy

The pillboxes on the beach
cannot get rid of their concrete.
At times a moribund general
arrives and strokes the loopholes.
Or tourists come to spend
five agonized minutes—
wind, sand, paper and urine:
the invasion goes on.

The Sea Battle

An American aircraft carrier
and a Gothic cathedral
simultaneously sank each other
in the middle of the Pacific.
To the last
the young curate played on the organ.
Now aeroplanes and angels hang in the air
and have nowhere to land.

Askese

Die Katze spricht.
Was spricht die Katze denn?
Du sollst mit einem spitzen Blei
die Bräute und den Schnee schattieren,
du sollst die graue Farbe lieben,
unter bewölktem Himmel sein.

Die Katze spricht.
Was spricht die Katze denn?
Du sollst dich mit dem Abendblatt,
in Sacktuch wie Kartoffeln kleiden,
und diesen Anzug immer wieder wenden
und nie in neuem Anzug sein.

Die Katze spricht.
Was spricht die Katze denn?
Du solltest die Marine streichen,
die Kirschen, Mohn und Nasenbluten,
auch jene Fahne sollst du streichen
und Asche auf Geranien streun.

Du sollst, so spricht die Katze weiter,
nur noch von Nieren, Milz und Leber,
von atemloser saurer Lunge,
vom Seich der Nieren, ungewässert,
von alter Milz und zäher Leber,
aus grauem Topf: so sollst du leben.

Und an die Wand, wo früher pausenlos
das grüne Bild das Grüne wiederkäute,
sollst du mit deinem spitzen Blei
Askese schreiben, schreib: Askese.
So spricht die Katze: Schreib Askese.

Askesis

The cat speaks.
And what does the cat say?
Thou shalt draw with sharpened pencil
brides of shade and shade of snow,
thou shalt love the colour grey
and be beneath a cloudy sky.

The cat speaks.
And what does the cat say?
Thou shalt be clad in the evening paper,
clad in sackcloth like potatoes,
and thou shalt turn this suit year out year in,
and in a new suit never be.

The cat speaks.
And what does the cat say?
Thou shouldst scratch the navy out;
cherries, poppy, bloody nose
thou shalt scratch out, that flag as well,
and daub geraniums with ash.

Thou, the cat goes on to say,
Shalt live on kidneys, spleen and liver,
lung that's out of breath and sour,
on urine of unsoaked kidneys,
old spleen and tough liver
out of a grey pot: live on that.

And on the wall, where earlier without pause
the ruminant green picture chewed its green,
thou shalt write with thy sharp pencil
this: Askesis; write: Askesis.
That's what the cat says: write Askesis.

43

Diana—oder die Gegenstände

Wenn sie mit rechter Hand
über die rechte Schulter in ihren Köcher greift,
stellt sie das linke Bein vor.

Als sie mich traf,
traf ihr Gegenstand meine Seele,
die ihr wie ein Gegenstand ist.

Zumeist sind es ruhende Gegenstände,
an denen sich montags
mein Knie aufschlägt.

Sie aber, mit ihrem Jagdschein,
läßt sich nur laufend
und zwischen Hunden fotografieren.

Wenn sie ja sagt und trifft,
trifft sie die Gegenstände der Natur
aber auch ausgestopfte.

Immer lehnte ich ab,
von einer schattenlosen Idee
meinen schattenwerfenden Körper verletzen zu lassen.

Doch du, Diana,
mit deinem Bogen
bist mir gegenständlich und haftbar.

Diana—or the Objects

When with her right hand she reaches
over her right shoulder into the quiver,
she puts forward her left leg.

When she hit me,
her object hit my soul
which is to her like an object.

Mostly it is objects resting
against which on Mondays
my knee smashes.

But she, with her hunting permit,
may be photographed only
running and among hounds.

When she says yes and hits,
she hits the objects in nature,
but also stuffed ones.

I have always refused
to let my shadow-casting body
be hurt by a shadowless idea.

But you, Diana,
with your bow,
are to me objective and answerable.

Ausverkauf

Ich habe alles verkauft.
Die Leute stiegen vier Treppen hoch,
klingelten zweimal, atemlos
und zahlten mir auf den Fußboden,
weil der Tisch schon verkauft war.

Während ich alles verkaufte,
enteigneten sie fünf oder sechs Straßen weiter
die besitzanzeigenden Fürwörter
und sägten den kleinen harmlosen Männern
den Schatten ab, den privaten.

Ich habe alles verkauft.
Bei mir ist nichts mehr zu holen.
Selbst meinen letzten winzigsten Genitiv,
den ich von früher her anhänglich aufbewahrte,
habe ich günstig verkaufen können.

Alles habe ich verkauft.
Den Stühlen machte ich Beine,
dem Schrank sprach ich das Recht ab,
die Betten stellte ich bloß—
ich legte mich wunschlos daneben.

Am Ende war alles verkauft.
Die Hemden kragen- und hoffnungslos,
die Hosen wußten zuviel,
einem rohen blutjungen Kotelett
schenkte ich meine Bratpfanne

und gleichfalls mein restliches Salz.

Sale

I've sold out, all I owned, the lot.
Four flights of stairs they came up,
rang the bell twice, out of breath,
and paid down their cash on the floor,
since the table too had been sold.

While I was selling it all,
five or six streets from here they expropriated
all the possessive pronouns
and sawed off the private shadows
of little innocuous men.

I've sold out, all I owned, the lot.
There's no more to be had from me.
Even my last and tiniest genitive,
a keepsake long treasured devoutly,
fetched a good price in the end.

All I owned is sold now, the lot.
My old chairs—I sent them packing.
The wardrobe—I gave it the sack.
The beds—I stripped them, exposed them
and lay down beside them, abstemious.

In the end all I'd owned had been sold.
The shirts were collarless, hopeless,
the trousers by now knew too much;
to a raw and blushing young cutlet
I made a gift of my frying-pan

and all that was left of my salt.

Kleine Aufforderung zum
grossen Mundaufmachen—oder
der Wasserspeier spricht

Wer jene Fäulnis,
die lange hinter der Zahnpaste lebte,
freigeben, ausatmen will,
muß seinen Mund aufmachen.

Wir wollen nun den Mund aufmachen,
die schlimmen Goldzähne,
die wir den Toten brachen und pflückten,
auf Ämtern abliefern.

Um dicke Väter
—jetzt, da auch wir schon Väter und immer dicker—
absetzen und ausspeien zu können,
muß man den Mund aufmachen;

wie unsere Kinder bei Zeiten
den Mund aufmachen, die große Fäulnis,
die schlimmen Goldzähne, die dicken Väter
ausspeien werden, absetzen werden.

**Little Address Calling for
a Great Opening of Mouths—
or the Gargoyle Speaks**

Whoever wishes
to release, to breathe out
that caries which long has lurked behind the toothpaste
has no choice but to open his mouth.

Now let us open our mouths,
go to offices and hand in
the bad gold teeth
which we broke and plucked from the dead.

Before you can hope to
depose, to spew out fat fathers—
now that we too are fathers and putting on fat—
you've no choice but to open your mouths;

just as our children in time will
open their mouths, will depose,
will spew out the great caries,
the bad gold teeth, the fat fathers.

Köche und Löffel

Und manche sagen: Koch ist Koch.
Neu, frischgewaschen und gestärkt,
im Schneefall und vor heller Wand
bleiben die Köche unbemerkt,
und nur der Löffel in der Hand
rührt uns, läßt niemanden vergessen:
Die Köche geben uns zu essen.

Wir sollten nicht von Suppen sprechen
—der Suppenkohl kann nicht dafür—
denn Hunger heißt nur, Vorwand für ein Bier,
und Überdruß leckt jedem Löffel Flächen
und sitzt und zählt die Schritte bis zur Tür.

Die Puppen überleben sich,
der Hahn stirbt vor dem Koch
und kräht woanders, dennoch zittern
in dieser Stadt manchmal die Scheiben.
Die Puppen überleben sich,
der Hahn stirbt vor dem Koch.

Es liegt am Fleisch, der Koch lebt nur im Geist.
Die Zeit vergeht, das Rindfleisch wird nicht weich,
wird später, wird im Schlaf noch dauern,
wird zwischen deinen Zähnen kauern;
es liegt am Fleisch, der Koch lebt nur im Geist.

Sie legten beide, jeder legte sich,
sie legten sich zusammen in den Löffel,
nur weil er hohl war, Schlaf vortäuschte,
—auch hohl war Vorwand und nur Widerspruch—
der Schlaf blieb kurz und kurz vorm Überkochen
hat beide, und ein jeder lag alleine,
derselbe Löffel abgeschöpft.

Chefs and Spoons

And some will say: a chef's a chef.
All newly laundered, starched and spry
in snowfall or against a wall
that's whitewashed, chefs escape the eye
and then the spoons they hold are all
that stirs us, leaves us in no doubt:
the things we eat, the chefs dish out.

I don't think we should talk of soup
—the cabbage stock is neither here nor there—
for hunger is mere pretext for a beer,
and glut licks large and small spoons out of shape
and sits and counts the paces to the door.

The dolls outlive themselves,
the rooster dies before the chef
and crows elsewhere, and yet at times
the window panes will shiver in this town.
The dolls outlive themselves,
the rooster dies before the chef.

Flesh is the cause, a chef lives but in spirit.
Time passes, but the beef is still not done,
will last till later, till you sleep,
between your teeth will creep and lurk;
flesh is the cause, a chef lives but in spirit.

They both lay down, each one of them lay down,
together in the spoon they both lay down,
for it was hollow and it promised sleep—
yet hollow too was pretext and mere contradiction—
their sleep was short and shortly before boiling over
both, and now each one lay alone,
the self-same spoon skimmed off.

Hier ist kein Tod, der nicht zum Löffel führt,
und keine Liebe, die nicht ausgehöhlt
an Löffeln leidet und im Löffel bebt,
sich dreht, worum dreht, da sich alles
mit Löffeln nur um Löffel dreht.

Bleib Löffel, geh.
Wem Löffel, Löffel führt wohin.
Wann Löffel, Löffel kam zu spät.
Wer rührt mich, rührt mich und wohin.
Über und über wen balbiert.
Bleib, Löffel, geh—und sag mir nicht wohin.

So lernst du langsam Löffel unterscheiden,
kannst dich in Schubladen nicht mehr vermeiden,
du löffelst mit und läßt dich gern vertauschen,
du gibst dich blechern, gleichst dich an,
hörst deinen Nachbarn, wolltest gar nicht lauschen,
doch Löffel liegt dem Löffel an.

No death is here but leads back to the spoon,
and no love here but, hollowed out, at last
suffers from spoons and trembles in the spoon,
revolves, revolves round what, since everything
with spoons revolves round spoons and only spoons.

Then stay, spoon, go.
To whom spoon, spoon leads where.
What time spoon, spoon was late.
Who stirs me, stirs me where.
Over and over cuts whose hair.
Then stay, spoon, go—and do not tell me where.

So gradually you learn to tell the spoons apart,
no longer can avoid yourself in drawers,
spoon with the rest and like to be mistaken,
act tinny and assimilate yourself,
can hear your neighbour, never meant to eavesdrop,
yet spoon fits into spoon, lies close to spoon.

Saturn

In diesem großen Haus
—von den Ratten,
die um den Abfluß wissen,
bis zu den Tauben,
die nichts wissen—
wohne ich und ahne vieles.

Kam spät nach Hause,
schloß mit dem Schlüssel
die Wohnung auf
und merkte beim Schlüsselsuchen,
daß ich einen Schlüssel brauche,
um bei mir einkehren zu können.

Hatte wohl Hunger,
aß noch ein Hühnchen
mit meinen Händen
und merkte beim Hühnchenessen,
daß ich ein kaltes und totes
Hühnchen aß.

Bückte mich dann,
zog beide Schuhe aus
und merkte beim Schuhausziehen,
daß wir uns bücken müssen,
wenn wir die Schuhe
ausziehen wollen.

Waagerecht lag ich,
rauchte die Zigarette
und war im Dunkeln gewiß,
daß jemand die Hand aufhielt,
als ich meiner Zigarette
die Asche abklopfte.

Saturn

In this big house—
from the rats
who know about the drains,
to the pigeons
who know nothing—
I live and suppose much.

Came home late,
opened the house
with my key
and noticed as I hunted for my key
that I needed a key
to enter my own home.

Was quite hungry,
ate a chicken
with my hands
and noticed as I ate the chicken
that I was eating a chicken
which was cold and dead.

Then stooped,
took off both shoes
and noticed as I took off my shoes
that we have to stoop
if we want to take
shoes off.

I lay horizontal,
smoked the cigarette,
and in the darkness was certain
that someone held out his open hand
when I knocked the ashes
from my cigarette.

Nachts kommt Saturn
und hält seine Hand auf.
Mit meiner Asche
putzt seine Zähne Saturn.
In seinen Rachen
werden wir steigen.

At night Saturn comes
and holds out his hand.
With my ashes, he
cleans his teeth, Saturn.
We shall climb
into his jaws.

NEW POEMS

Ausgefragt

Nach grossem und nach kleingemünztem Zorn,—
beliebtes Beispiel, dem man Zucker gab,—
nach soviel Damals und dem Salto
auf einem Hochseil, das periodenlang
gespannt war,—Arbeit ohne Netz,—
will, will ich, will ich ganz und gar . . .
Wie sieht es aus?—Es sah schon schlimmer aus.
Du hattest Glück?—Es lag am Köder.
Und was hast du gemacht seitdem?
In Büchern steht, wie es sich besser machte.
Ich meine, was hast du getan?
Ich war dagegen. Immer schon dagegen.
Und wurdest schuldig?—Nein. Ich tat ja nichts.
Und hast erkannt, was sich erkennen liess?
Ja. Ich erkannte Gummi mit der Faust.

Und deine Hoffnung?—Log die Wüsten grün.
Und deine Wut?—Sie klirrt als Eis im Glas.
Die Scham?—Wir grüssen uns von fern.
Dein grosser Plan?—Zahlt sich zur Hälfte aus.
Hast du vergessen?—Neuerdings, mein Kopf.
Und die Natur?—Oft fahr ich dran vorbei.
Die Menschen?—Seh ich gern im Film.
Sie sterben wieder.—Ja. Ich las davon . . .
Wer seift mich ab? Mir ist mein Rücken
so fern wie—Nein!—
ich will nicht mehr vergleichen
und widerkäuen, Silben stechen
und warten, bis die Galle schreibt.
Ist es jetzt besser?—Es sieht besser aus.
Soll ich noch fragen?—Frag mich aus.

Questioned

About the large and the small coin of anger,—
popular instance that was fed with sugar,—
after so much At That Time and the leap
up on a tightrope that whole periods long
was tautened,—work without a net,—
I will, with all my heart, I will . . .
    How do things look?—They have looked worse.
    You were in luck?—It was the bait.
    And what have you been doing since?
    In books you'll find out how it should be done.
    I mean, what have you done?
    I was against it. Always, from the start.
    And so are guilty?—No, since I did nothing.
    And you have learnt all that there was to learn?
    Yes. With my fist I learned what rubber is.

    And hope? Your hope?—It lied the deserts green.
    Your rage?—As ice it clatters in the glass.
    And shame?—We greet each other, from a distance.
    Your major project?—Isn't worth all that much.
    Have you forgotten?—Lately, yes, my head.
    And nature?—Often I drive past it.
    Your fellow men?—I like to see them filmed.
    Once more they're dying.—Yes, I've read about it.
Who soaps and washes me? My back feels far
From me as—No!—
Enough of that. Enough of similes,
chewing the cud and splitting hairs,
of waiting for my gall to write.
    Well, is that better?—It looks better now.
    More questions?—Yes, continue. Pump me dry.

Zwischen Greise gestellt

Wie sie mit neunzig noch lügen
und ihren Tod vertagen,
bis er Legende wird.

In die fleckigen Hände
frühaufstehender Greise
wurde die Welt gelegt.

Die vielgefältete Macht
und der Faltenwurf alter Haut
verachten die Glätte.

Wir, zwischen Greise gestellt,
kauen die Nägel knapp,
wir wachsen nicht nach.

Hart, weise und gütig
dauern sie in Askese
und überleben uns bald.

Placed amid Old Men

How at ninety they still lie
   and put off their dying
      till it's a legend.

Into the mottled hands
   of old men who rise early
      the world was laid.

Their many times folded power
   and the folds of old skin
      despise what is smooth.

Placed amid old men, we
   bite our nails till they're spare,
      we make no new growth.

Hard, wise and kind
   they last ascetically
      and soon will outlive us.

Ehe

Wir haben Kinder, das zählt bis zwei.
Meistens gehen wir in verschiedene Filme.
Vom Auseinanderleben sprechen die Freunde.
Doch meine und Deine Interessen
berühren sich immer noch
an immer den gleichen Stellen.
Nicht nur die Frage nach den Manschettenknöpfen.
Auch Dienstleistungen:
Halt mal den Spiegel.
Glühbirnen auswechseln.
Etwas abholen.
Oder Gespräche, bis alles besprochen ist.
Zwei Sender, die manchmal gleichzeitig
auf Empfang gestellt sind.
Soll ich abschalten?
Erschöpfung lügt Harmonie.
Was sind wir uns schuldig? Das.
Ich mag das nicht: Deine Haare im Klo.
Aber nach elf Jahren noch Spass an der Sache.
Ein Fleisch sein bei schwankenden Preisen.
Wir denken sparsam in Kleingeld.
Im Dunkeln glaubst Du mir alles.
Aufribbeln und Neustricken.
Gedehnte Vorsicht.
Dankeschönsagen.
Nimm Dich zusammen.
Dein Rasen vor unserem Haus.
Jetzt bist Du wieder ironisch.
Lach doch darüber.
Hau doch ab, wenn Du kannst.
Unser Hass ist witterungsbeständig.

Marriage

We have children, that counts up to two.
We usually go to different films.
It's friends who talk of our drifting apart.
But your interests and mine
still touch, at the same points always.
Not only the question about cufflinks.
Little services too:
Just hold that mirror.
Change the bulbs.
Fetch something.
Or discussions, till everything is discussed.
Two stations that at times
are both tuned in to receive.
Shall I turn myself off?
Exhaustion simulates harmony.
What do we owe each other? That.
I don't like that—your hairs in the john.
But after eleven years the thing is still fun.
To be one flesh when prices fluctuate.
We think thriftily, in small coin.
In the dark you believe all I say.
Unpicking and knitting anew.
A stretched cautiousness.
Saying thank you.
Pull yourself together.
That lawn of yours in our garden.
Now you're being ironic again.
Why don't you laugh about it?
Clear out, then, if you can.
Our hatred is weatherproof.

Doch manchmal, zerstreut, sind wir zärtlich.
Die Zeugnisse der Kinder
müssen unterschrieben werden.
Wir setzen uns von der Steuer ab.
Erst übermorgen ist Schluss.
Du. Ja Du. Rauch nicht so viel.

But sometimes, distrait, we are tender.
The children's reports
have to be signed.
    We deduct each other from income tax.
    Not till the day after tomorrow will it be over.
    You. Yes, you. Don't smoke so much.

Advent

Wenn Onkel Dagobert wieder die Trompeten vertauscht,
und wir katalytisches Jericho mit Bauklötzen spielen,
weil das Patt der Eltern
oder das Auseinanderrücken im Krisenfall
den begrenzten Krieg,
also die Schwelle vom Schlafzimmer zur Eskalation,
weil Weihnachten vor der Tür steht,
nicht überschreiten will,
    wenn Onkel Dagobert wieder was Neues,
    die Knusper—Kneisschen—Maschine
    und ähnliche Mehrzweckwaffen Peng! auf den Markt wirft,
    bis eine Stunde später Rickeracke . . . Puff . . . Plops!
der konventionelle, im Kinderzimmer lokalisierte Krieg
sich unorthodox hochschaukelt,
und die Eltern,
weil die Weihnachtseinkäufe
nur begrenzte Entspannung erlauben,
und Tick, Track und Trick,—
das sind Donald Ducks Neffen,—
wegen nichts Schild und Schwert vertauscht haben,
ihre gegenseitige, zweite und abgestufte,
ihre erweiterte Abschreckung aufgeben,
nur noch minimal flüstern, Bitteschön sagen,
wenn Onkel Dagobert wieder mal mit den Panzerknackern
und uns, wenn wir brav sind, doomsday spielt,
weil wir alles vom Teller wegessen müssen,
weil die Kinder in Indien Hunger haben
und weniger Spielzeug und ABC-Waffen,
die unsere tägliche Vorwärtsverteidigung
vom Wohnzimmer bis in die Hausbar tragen,
in die unsere Eltern das schöne Kindergeld stecken,
bis sie über dreckige Sachen lachen,

Advent

When Uncle Dagobert again swaps trumpets
and we play catalytic Jericho with wooden bricks
because the stalemate between our parents
or their disengagement in crisis periods
does not want to exceed
limited war,
that is, the threshold between bedroom and escalation,
because Christmas is at the door,
    when Uncle Dagobert again throws something new,
    the crackle and crunch machine
    and such-like all-purpose weapons Bang! on to the market
    till an hour later Whizzbuzz . . . Puff . . . Plop!
    conventional war, localized in the nursery,
    unorthodoxly flares up
    and our parents
    because the Christmas shopping
    permits only limited relaxation of tension
    and Huey, Dewey and Louie,—
    those are Donald Duck's nephews,—
    for no reason have swapped shields and swords,
    give up their reciprocal, second
    and gradual deterrent, only
    minimally whisper now, and say please,
when Uncle Dagobert again with the safe-crackers
and with us, if we're good, plays doomsday,
because we have to eat up everything on our plates
because the children in India go hungry
and have fewer toys and ABC weapons
which carry our daily forward defence
from the drawing-room up to the house bar
on which our parents spend all that lovely children's allowance
until they laugh about their dirty jokes,

kontrolliert explodieren
und sich eigenhändig,
wie wir unseren zerlegbaren Heuler,
zusammensetzen können,
    wenn ich mal gross und nur halb so reich
    wie Onkel Dagobert bin,
    werde ich alle Eltern, die überall rumstehen
    und vom Kinder anschaffen und Kinder abschaffen reden,
    mit einem richtigen spasmischen Krieg überziehen
    und mit Trick, Track und Tick,—
    das sind die Neffen von Donald Duck,—
    eine Familie planen,
    wo bös lieb und lieb bös ist
    und wir mit Vierradantrieb in einem Land-Rover
    voller doll absoluter Lenkwaffen
    zur Schule dürfen,
    damit wir den ersten Schlag führen können;
denn Onkel Dagobert sagt immer wieder:
Die minimale Abschreckung hat uns bis heute,—
und Heiligabend rückt immer näher,—
keinen Entenschritt weiter gebracht.

restrainedly explode
and with their own hands, as we can
our make-it-yourself siren,
can put themselves together again,
    when I'm grown up and half as rich
    as Uncle Dagobert,
    I shall plunge all those parents who everywhere
    stand around and talk of getting children
    and getting rid of children, into a real spasmic war
    and with Huey, Dewey and Louie,—
    those are Donald Duck's nephews,—
    I shall plan a family
    in which naughty is good and good naughty
    and we can go to school
    with a four-wheel drive in a Land Rover
    full of smashing all-in guided missiles
    so that we can strike the first blow;
for Uncle Dagobert is always saying:
Up to now the minimal deterrent,—
and Christmas Eve is drawing closer and closer,—
hasn't got us a duck's step further, has it now?

Plötzliche Angst

Wenn sich im Sommer bei östlichem Wind
Septemberstaub rührt und in verspäteter Zeitung
die Kommentare Mystisches streifen,

wenn sich die Mächte umbetten wollen
und zur Kontrolle neue Geräte
öffentlich zeugen dürfen,

wenn um den Fussball Urlauber zelten
und der Nationen verspielter Blick
grosse Entscheidungen spiegelt,

wenn Zahlenkolonnen den Schlaf erzwingen
und durch die Träume getarnter Feind
atmet, auf Ellbogen robbt,

wenn in Gesprächen immer das gleiche Wort
aufgespart in der Hinterhand bleibt
und ein Zündhölzlein Mittel zum Schreck wird,

wenn sich beim Schwimmen in Rückenlage
himmelwärts nur der Himmel türmt,
suchen die Ängstlichen rasch das Ufer,

liegt plötzliche Angst in der Luft.

Sudden Fright

When in summer in an easterly wind
  September dust whirls and in the belated paper
    editorials are almost mystical,

when the powers want to change beds
  and are allowed to beget openly
    new instruments for control,

when around footballs holiday makers camp
  and the playful glance of the nations
    mirrors weighty decisions,

when columns of figures put one to sleep
  and through dreams a camouflaged enemy
    breathes, and crawls nearer,

when in conversations always the same word
  is backhandedly held in reserve
    and a match can strike terror,

when from the backstroke position in swimming
  skyward only the sky seems to tower,
    frightened people hurry back to the shore,

a sudden fright hangs in the air.

König Lear

In der Halle,
in jeder Hotelhalle,
in einem eingesessenen Sessel,
Klub-, Leder-, doch niemals Korbsessel,
zwischen verfrühten Kongressteilnehmern
und leeren Sesseln, die Anteil haben,
selten, dann mit Distanz gegrüsst,
sitzt er, die von Kellnern umsegelte Insel,
und vergisst nichts.

Diese Trauer findet an sich Geschmack
und lacht mit zwölf Muskeln einerseits.
Viel hört er nicht aber alles
und widerlegt den Teppich.
Die Stukkatur denkt er weg
und stemmt seine Brauen gegen.
Bis sich ihr Blattgold löst,
sprechen Barockengel vor.
Die Kirche schickt Spitzel;
ihm fehlen Komparsen.
Vergeblich ahmen zuviele Spiegel ihn nach.
Seine Töchter sind Anekdoten.

Im Hotel Sacher wird nach Herrn Kortner verlangt.
Herr Kortner lässt sagen, er sei auf der Probe.
In der Halle, in seinem Sessel, stellt jemand sich tot
und trifft sich mit Kent auf der Heide.

King Lear

In the hall
in any hotel hall
in a chair that sags with long use,
club, leather but never basket chair,
amid premature participants in congresses
and empty armchairs that play their part,
rarely addressed and, if so, with reserve,
he sits,
an island skirted by cruising waiters,
and forgets nothing.

This grief takes pleasure in itself
and laughs with twelve muscles on the one side.
He does not hear much but everything
and refutes the carpet.
His mind rips off the stucco work
and his eyebrows push it away.
Till their gold leaf peels off
baroque angels present themselves.
The church sends informers;
what he lacks is walk-ons.
In vain too many mirrors copy him.
His daughters are anecdotes.

In Hotel Sacher Herr Kortner is paged.
Herr Kortner is busy rehearsing, he has them say.
In the hall, in his armchair, someone acts dead
and goes to meet Kent on the heath.

Vom Rest unterm Nagel

Wovon erzählen, immer noch vom Knopf
und Bodensatz, der übrig blieb,
von Aschenbechern, Sound and Light,
was übrig blieb, was überblieb,
vom Zinsertrag der kleinen Konten
und von der Zeit, die uns geblieben?

Wovon erzählen, von der Liebe?
Wovon? Noch immer von der Liebe?
Wovon, als ob nur Liebe zählt
und jeder nicht mit seinem Kot allein
auf jedem Abtritt einzeln steht,
mit Fingernägeln: ganz allein.

Das kratzt sich offen, heilt sich nicht
und speichert Reste unterm Nagel:
ich trenn mich nicht, ich putz sie nicht
und weise alle harten Instrumente
zurück: denn Liebe geht mit Geiz
zu Tisch zu Bett und wäscht sich nicht.

Wovon, wenn von der Liebe nicht?
Vom Vorrat, wenn wir fleissig sind,
vom fetten schwarzen abverdienten Rest
will ich erzählen, wenn wir fertig sind
und unsre Nägel, zweimalzehn,
vom Augentauschen dreckig sind.

Of the Residue under Our Nails

Talk about what now, still about the button
and dregs, deposits left behind,
about the ashtrays, Sound and Light,
whatever stayed, was left behind,
the interest rate on small accounts,
about the time we still have left?

Talk about what now, about love?
What? About love still? Even now?
Of that? As though love only counted
And every one of us were not alone
each morning only with his turd,
with fingernails, and quite alone.

This is scratched open, does not heal,
and under nails hoards residues:
I will not part with, will not clean them
and I refuse sharp instruments,
all kinds: for love with avarice goes
to meals to bed and does not wash.

Well, of what else then, if not love?
Of savings, if we work our stint,
of that black, greasy hard-earned residue
I'll talk when we have finished work
and when those nails of ours, twice ten,
are foul with intercourse of eyes.

Offenes Feuer

Ein leeres Haus im Rücken,
und die Gewissheit trocknender Strümpfe;
draussen mühen sich ab altbekannte Gewitter.

Mit imprägnierten Gedanken
in fremder Glut, später in Asche
stochern; denn die erwärmte Seite hat recht.

Genüsse und schöne Gespräche
mit dem erregten schreckhaften Holz;
ich lasse mich leicht überreden.

Das lebt vor sich hin, bis. Mach,
nun mach schon die Tür zu.
Drinnen wird alles wirklich.

Die früher bewohnten Kamine
wurden schon gestern geräumt.
Morgen, kopfunten, hängt kalter Rauch.

Open Fire

An empty house behind me,
  and the certainty of drying socks;
    outside, familiar thunderstorms exert themselves.

With waterproofed thoughts
  to poke about in a strange ardour, later
    in ashes; for the warm side is in the right.

Pleasures and fine conversations
  with the excited timorous wood:
    I am easily persuaded.

This quietly lives on, until. Shut,
  will you please shut the door.
    Inside, all becomes real.

The previously inhabited fireplaces
  were already cleaned out yesterday.
    Tomorrow, head down, cold smoke will hang.

Schlaflos

Mein Atem verfehlte das Nadelöhr.
Jetzt muss ich zählen
und heimwärts blättern treppab.

Aber die Kriechgänge
münden in Wassergräben,
in denen Kaulquappen . . .
Zähl doch mal nach.

Meine Rückspule plappert ihr drittes Jahrzehnt.
Das Bett geht auf Reisen. Und überall legt
der Zoll seine Hand auf: Was führen sie mit?

Drei Strümpfe, fünf Schuhe, ein Nebelgerät.—
Mehrsprachig werden sie nachgezählt:
die Sterne, die Schafe, die Panzer, die Stimmen . . .
Ein Zwischenergebnis wird ausgezählt.

Sleepless

My breath missed the needle's eye.
Now I must count
and homeward leaf down the stairs.

But the crawling forays
end in watery ditches,
in which tadpoles . . .
Count up again.

My playback reel gabbles its third decade.
The bed leaves for a journey. And everywhere
The Customs interpose: What's in your luggage?

Three socks, five shoes, a fog machine.—
In several languages they are counted up:
the stars, the sheep, the tanks, the voices . . .
A provisional sum is counted out.

Liebe

Das ist es:
Der bargeldlose Verkehr.
Die immer zu kurze Decke.
Der Wackelkontakt.

Hinter dem Horizont suchen.
Im Laub mit vier Schuhen rascheln
und in Gedanken Barfüsse reiben.
Herzen vermieten und mieten;
oder im Zimmer mit Dusche und Spiegel,
im Leihwagen, Kühler zum Mond,
wo immer die Unschuld absteigt
und ihr Programm verbrennt,
fistelt das Wort
jedesmal anders und neu.

Heute, vor noch geschlossener Kasse,
knisterten Hand in Hand
der gedrückte Greis und die zierliche Greisin.
Der Film versprach Liebe.

Love

That's it:
The cashless commerce.
The blanket always too short.
The loose connection.

To search behind the horizon.
To brush fallen leaves with four shoes
and in one's mind to rub bare feet.
To let and to rent hearts;
or in a room with shower and mirror,
in a hired car, bonnet facing the moon,
wherever innocence stops
and burns its programme,
the word in falsetto sounds
different and new each time.

Today, in front of a box office not yet open,
hand in hand crackled
the hangdog old man and the dainty old woman.
The film promised love.

Dreht euch nicht um

Geh nicht in den Wald,
im Wald ist der Wald.
Wer im Wald geht,
Bäume sucht,
wird im Wald nicht mehr gesucht.

Hab keine Angst,
die Angst riecht nach Angst.
Wer nach Angst riecht,
den riechen
Helden, die wie Helden riechen.

Trink nicht vom Meer,
das Meer schmeckt nach mehr.
Wer vom Meer trinkt,
hat fortan
nur noch Durst auf Ocean.

Bau dir kein Haus,
sonst bist du zuhaus.
Wer zuhaus ist,
wartet auf
spät Besuch und macht auf.

Schreib keinen Brief,
Brief kommt ins Archiv.
Wer den Brief schreibt,
unterschreibt,
was von ihm einst überbleibt.

Don't Turn Round

Don't go into the wood,
in the wood is the wood.
Whoever walks in the wood,
looks for trees,
will not be looked for later in the wood.

Have no fear,
fear smells of fear.
Whoever smells of fear
will be smelled out
by heroes who smell like heroes.

Don't drink from the sea,
the sea tastes of more sea.
Whoever drinks from the sea
henceforth feels
a thirst only for oceans.

Don't build a home,
or you'll be at home.
Whoever is at home
waits for
late callers and opens the door.

Don't write a letter,
letters that vex us end up in Texas.
Whoever writes the letter
lends his name
to the posthumous paper game.

Platzangst

Mama. Sie kommen auf mich zu
und knacken mit den Handgelenken,
die Söhne aus zu gutem Haus.

So wohlerzogen nimmt Gewalt
den Anlauf, nett, studentenhaft,
mit Kussmundfragen: Glauben Sie?
ein nackter Finger: Hoffen Sie?
die Drohung zielt, zum Schlips gebunden,
als Zusatzfrage: Lieben Sie?

Jetzt lockern sie den Knoten, jetzt:
Mitesser überlebensgross.
Die Söhne aus zu gutem Haus.

Es ist so schön hier, auch bei Regen.
An Zigaretten glaub ich immer noch.
Mein Schnittlauch grünt, die Hoffnung auch.
Und manchmal, wenn ich mich zerstreue,
kehrt mich die Liebe mit Geduld aufs Blech.

Mama. Es hat sich Heiterkeit
verflogen und ist überfällig.
Eng wird es zwischen Ideologen
und Söhnen aus zu gutem Haus.
Sie kommen näher. Ich will raus.

Claustrophobia

Mother. They're coming up to me
and ominously crack their wrists,
those boys from families too good.

So well brought up does violence
run to the start, so public school,
so nice, caressing: Do you believe?
a naked finger: Do you hope?
the threat, a necktie neatly knotted,
aims as a supplement: Do you love?

And now the knot is loosened, now:
blackheads much more than life-size, bloated.
Those boys from families too good.

A lovely place, even in rainy weather.
I still believe in cigarettes, don't you?
My chives are green and thriving, so is hope.
And sometimes, when I seek distraction,
love sweeps me on the dustpan patiently.

Mother. This cheerfulness has flown
too far and now is overdue.
They're closing up—the ideologists
and boys from families too good.
They're coming nearer. Let me out.

Hymne

So kompliziert wie eine Nachtigall,
so blechern wie,
gutmütig wie,
so knitterfrei, althergebracht,
so grün ernst sauer, so durchwachsen,
so ebenmässig,
so behaart,
so nah dem Wasser, windgerecht,
so feuerfest, oft umgegraben,
so kinderleicht, zerlesen wie,
so neu und knarrend, teuer wie,
so unterkellert, häuslich wie,
so leicht verloren, blankgegriffen,
so dünn geblasen, schneegekühlt,
so eigenhändig, mündig wie,
so herzlos wie,
so sterblich wie,
so einfach wie meine Seele.

Hymn

As complicated as a nightingale,
as tinny as,
kind-hearted as,
as crease-proof, as traditional,
as green grave sour, as streaky,
as symmetrical,
as hairy,
as near the water, true to the wind,
as fireproof, frequently turned over,
as childishly easy, well-thumbed as,
as new and creaking, expensive as,
as deeply cellared, domestic as,
as easily lost, shiny with use,
as thinly blown, as snow-chilled as,
as independent, as mature,
as heartless as,
as mortal as,
as simple as my soul.

Orpheus

Weil ich mich damals zum Publikum zählte,
nahm ich Platz in der siebzehnten Reihe.
So, die Hände überm Programm,
hielt ich es aus bis kurz nach der Pause:

den Kapellmeister strich ich durch,
dem Klavier ins Gebiss, der Flöte ein Auge
weg und das Blech gefüllt,—womit denn?—mit Blei.
Es galt, die Hälfte aller Instrumente zu enthaaren.

Wer schnitt mir damals den Film ab?
Platzanweiser bekamen Gewalt,
warfen mich Geigen vor, Hemdbrüsten,
was von Noten schwarz-weiss lebt, liniert.

Die Harfenistin, trotzdem ein Weib,
beugte sich über mich, trug ein mildtätig Kleid.
So ging ich in ihre Saiten ein,
verstehe mich nur noch auf Finger:

Wohlklang, ich überhöre mich, hüte mich,
nach ihrem Programm zu verlangen.

Orpheus

Because at that time I thought myself part of the public
I took a seat in the seventeenth row.
Like that, my hands on the programme,
I stuck it out till shortly after the intermission.

I cancelled the conductor with one bold stroke,
aimed at the piano's denture, put out one eye
of the flute and filled the brass—with what, then?—with lead.
To depilate half the instruments, that's what was needed.

Who cut my film at that time?
Ushers were given power,
hurled me down before violins, shirtfronts,
all that of notes lives black and white, ruled.

The harpist, a woman all the same,
bent over me, wore a charitable dress.
So I passed over into her strings,
an adept now only in fingers:

Euphony, I listen to myself, beware
of asking for her programme.

Der Dampfkessel-Effekt

Immer zum Zischen bereit.
Schneller gezischt als gedacht.
Nicht mehr mit Fäusten,
zischend wird argumentiert.
Bald wird es heissen:
Er wurde zu Tode gezischt.
Aber noch lebt er und spricht.
Auf seine Frage gab Zischen Antwort.
Seht dieses Volk, im Zischen geeint.
Zischoman. Zischoplex. Zischophil.
Denn das Zischen macht gleich,
kostet wenig und wärmt.
Aber es kostete wessen Geld,
diese Elite, geistreich und zischend,
heranzubilden.
Als wollte Dampfablassen
den nächstliegenden Nero bewegen,
jeweils den Daumen zu senken.
Pfeifen ist schön. Nicht jeder kann pfeifen.
Dieses jedoch, anonym,
macht ängstlich und lässt befürchten . . .

The Steam Boiler Effect

Always ready to hiss.
Sooner hissed than thought.
No longer with fists
people argue, but hissing.
Soon they will say:
He was hissed to death.
But still he's alive and speaks.
His questions were answered by hisses.
Look at this people, united in hissing.
Hissomaniac. Hissoplex. Hissophile.
For hissing is a leveller,
costs little and keeps warm.
But it costs whose money,
to train
this élite, witty and hissing.
As though letting off steam
could move the local Nero
to the thumb-down sign every time.
Whistling is fine. Not anyone can whistle.
But this thing, anonymous,
is worrying and makes one fear . . .

In Ohnmacht gefallen

Wir lesen Napalm und stellen Napalm uns vor.
Da wir uns Napalm nicht vorstellen können,
lesen wir über Napalm, bis wir uns mehr
unter Napalm vorstellen können.
Jetzt protestieren wir gegen Napalm.
Nach dem Frühstück, stumm,
auf Fotos sehen wir, was Napalm vermag.
Wir zeigen uns grobe Raster
und sagen: Siehst du, Napalm.
Das machen sie mit Napalm.
Bald wird es preiswerte Bildbände
mit besseren Fotos geben,
auf denen deutlicher wird,
was Napalm vermag.
Wir kauen Nägel und schreiben Proteste.
Aber es gibt, so lesen wir,
Schlimmeres als Napalm.
Schnell protestieren wir gegen Schlimmeres.
Unsere berechtigten Proteste, die wir jederzeit
verfassen falten frankieren dürfen, schlagen zu Buch.
Ohnmacht, an Gummifassaden erprobt.
Ohnmacht legt Platten auf: ohnmächtige Songs.
Ohne Macht mit Guitarre.—
Aber feinmaschig und gelassen
wirkt sich draussen die Macht aus.

Powerless, with a Guitar

We read napalm and imagine napalm.
Since we cannot imagine napalm
we read about napalm until
by napalm we can imagine more.
Now we protest against napalm.
　　After breakfast, silent,
　　we see in photographs what napalm can do.
　　We show each other coarse screen prints
　　and say: there you are, napalm.
　　They do that with napalm.
Soon there'll be cheap picture books
with better photographs
which will show more clearly
what napalm can do.
We bite our nails and write protests.
　　But, we read, there are
　　worse things than napalm.
　　Quickly we protest against worse things.
　　Our well-founded protests, which at any time
　　we may compose fold stamp, mount up.
Impotence, tried out on rubber façades.
Impotence puts records on: impotent songs.
Powerless, with a guitar.—
But outside, finely meshed
and composed, power has its way.

Irgendwas machen

Da können wir doch nicht zusehen.
Wenn wir auch nichts verhindern,
wir müssen uns deutlich machen.
(Mach doch was. Mach doch was.
Irgendwas. Mach doch was.)
Zorn, Ärger und Wut suchten sich ihre Adjektive.
Der Zorn nannte sich gerecht.
Bald sprach man vom alltäglichen Ärger.
Die Wut fiel in Ohnmacht: ohnmächtige Wut.
Ich spreche vom Protestgedicht
und gegen das Protestgedicht.
(Einmal sah ich Rekruten beim Eid
mit Kreuzfingern hinterrücks abschwören.)
Ohnmächtig protestiere ich gegen ohnmächtige Proteste.
Es handelt sich um Oster-, Schweige- und Friedensmärsche.
Es handelt sich um die hundert guten Namen
unter sieben richtigen Sätzen.
Es handelt sich um Guitarren und ähnliche
die Schallplatte fördernde Protestinstrumente.
Ich rede vom hölzernen Schwert und vom fehlenden Zahn,
vom Protestgedicht.

Wie Stahl seine Konjunktur hat, hat Lyrik ihre Konjunktur.
Aufrüstung öffnet Märkte für Antikriegsgedichte.
Die Herstellungskosten sind gering.
Man nehme: ein Achtel gerechten Zorn,
zwei Achtel alltäglichen Ärger
und fünf Achtel, damit sie vorschmeckt, ohnmächtige Wut.
Denn mittelgrosse Gefühle gegen den Krieg
sind billig zu haben
und seit Troja schon Ladenhüter.
(Mach doch was. Mach doch was.
Irgendwas. Mach doch was.)

Do Something

We can't just look on.
Even if we can't stop anything
we must say what we think.
(Do something. Do something.
Anything. Do something, then.)
Indignation, annoyance, rage looked for their adjectives.
Indignation called itself righteous.
Soon people spoke of everyday annoyance.
Rage fell into impotence: impotent rage.
I speak of the protest poem
and against the protest poem.
(Once I saw recruits taking the oath
unswear it behind their backs with crossed fingers.)
Impotently I protest against impotent protests.
What I mean is Easter, silence and peace marches.
What I mean is the hundred good names
underneath seven true sentences.
What I mean is guitars and similar
protest instruments conducive to records.
I speak of the wooden sword and the missing tooth,
of the protest poem.

Just as steel has its booms, so poetry has its booms.
Rearmament opens markets for anti-war poems.
The cost of production is low.
Take an eighth of righteous indignation,
two eighths of everyday annoyance
and five eighths—to heighten that flavour—of impotent rage.
For medium-sized feelings against the war
are cheaply obtained
and have been shopsoiled ever since Troy.
(Do something. Do something.
Anything. Do something, then.)

Man macht sich Luft: schon verraucht der gerechte Zorn.
Der kleine alltägliche Ärger lässt die Ventile zischen.
Ohnmächtige Wut entlädt sich, füllt einen Luftballon,
der steigt und steigt, wird kleiner und kleiner, ist weg.
Sind Gedichte Atemübungen?
Wenn sie diesen Zweck erfüllen,—und ich frage,
prosaisch wie mein Grossvater, nach dem Zweck,—
dann ist Lyrik Therapie.
Ist das Gedicht eine Waffe?
Manche, überarmiert, können kaum laufen.
Sie müssen das Unbehagen an Zuständen
als Vehikel benutzen:
sie kommen ans Ziel, sie kommen ans Ziel:
zuerst ins Feuilleton und dann in die Anthologie:
Die Napalm-Metapher und ihre Abwandlungen
im Protestgedicht der sechziger Jahre.
Es handelt sich um Traktatgedichte.
Gerechter Zorn zählt Elend und Terror auf.
Alltäglicher Ärger findet den Reim auf fehlendes Brot.
Ohnmächtige Wut macht atemlos von sich reden.
(Mach doch was. Mach doch was . . .)
Dabei gibt es Hebelgesetze.
Sie aber kreiden ihm an, dem Stein,
er wolle sich nicht bewegen.
Tags drauf ködert der hilflose Stil berechtigter Proteste
den treffsicheren Stil glatter Dementis.
Weil sie in der Sache zwar jeweils recht haben,
sich im Detail aber allzu leicht irren,
distanzieren sich die Unterzeichner
halblaut von den Verfassern und ihren Protesten.
(Nicht nur Diebe kaufen sich Handschuhe.)
Was übrig bleibt: zählebige Missverständnisse

One lets off steam: already righteous indignation goes up in smoke.
The small everyday annoyance makes the safety valves hiss.
Impotent rage discharges itself, fills a balloon with gas,
this rises, rises, grows smaller and smaller, is gone.
Are poems breathing exercises?
If that is their function,—and prosaic
as my grandfather, I ask what their function is—
then poetry is therapy.
Is a poem a weapon?
Some, too heavily armed, can hardly walk.
They have to use their dissatisfaction with circumstances
as a vehicle:
they reach their destination, they can hit the mark:
first the weekly paper, then the anthology:
The napalm metaphor and its permutations
in the protest poem of the 'sixties.
I mean poems that are tracts.
Righteous indignation enumerates terrors and miseries.
Everyday annoyance discovers the rhyme for no bread.
Impotent rage sets people talking breathlessly about itself.
(Do something. Do something . . .)
There are laws of leverage.
But they hold it against the stone
that it will not budge.
Next day the helpless style of well-founded protest
acts as a bait for the well-aimed style of smooth refutation.
Since in the cause they are always right
but all too easily slip up over details
the signatories tacitly half-dissociate themselves
from the authors and from their protests.
(Not only burglars buy gloves.)
What remains is: resilient misunderstandings

zitieren einander. Fehlerhafte Berichtigungen
lernen vom Meerschweinchen
und vermehren sich unübersichtlich.

Da erbarmt sich der Stein und tut so,
als habe man ihn verrückt:
während Zorn, Ärger und Wut einander ins Wort fallen,
treten die Spezialisten der Macht
lächelnd vor Publikum auf. Sie halten fundierte
                              Vorträge
über den Preis, den die Freiheit fordert;
über Napalm und seine abschreckende Wirkung;
über berechtigte Proteste und die erklärliche Wut.
Das alles ist erlaubt.
Da die Macht nur die Macht achtet,
darf solange ohnmächtig protestiert werden,
bis nicht mehr, weil der Lärm stört,
protestiert werden darf.—
Wir aber verachten die Macht.
Wir sind nicht mächtig, beteuern wir uns.
Ohne Macht gefallen wir uns in Ohnmacht.
Wir wollen die Macht nicht; sie aber hat uns.—
Nun fühlt sich der gerechte Zorn missverstanden.
Der alltägliche Ärger mündet in Schweigemärsche,
die zuvor angemeldet und genehmigt wurden.
Im Kreis läuft die ohnmächtige Wut.
Das fördert den gleichfalls gerechten Zorn
verärgerter Polizisten:
ohnmächtige Wut wird handgreiflich.
Die Faust wächst sich zum Kopf aus
und denkt in Tiefschlägen Leberhaken knöchelhart.
(Mach doch was. Mach doch was . . .)
Das alles macht Schule und wird von der Macht

quote one another. Erroneous corrections
learn from guinea pigs
how to breed so that no one keeps track.

The stone takes pity and acts
as though it had been moved:
while indignation, annoyance and rage interrupt one another,
the specialists in power
appear smiling in front of the public. They make well-informed
                                        speeches
about the price demanded for freedom:
about napalm and its deterrent effects;
about well-founded protests and understandable rage.
All this is permitted.
Since power respects only power
impotent protest is allowed to carry on
until, because the noise is disturbing,
protest is no longer allowed.—
But we despise power.
We are not powerful, we keep assuring each other.
Without power we enjoy our impotence.
We do not want power; but power has us.—
Now righteous indignation feels misunderstood.
Our everyday annoyance ends in silence marches
that have first been announced and permitted.
Our impotent rage runs around in circles.
This provokes the equally righteous indignation
of angered policemen:
impotent rage becomes aggressive.
The fist grows into a head
and thinks in terms of low blows hooks to the liver knuckle-hard.
(Do something. Do something . . .)
All this becomes institutionalized, and by power

gestreichelt geschlagen subventioniert.
Schon setzt der Stein, der bewegt werden wollte,
unbewegt Moos an.
Geht das so weiter?—Im Kreis schon.
Was sollen wir machen?—Nicht irgendwas.
Wohin mit der Wut?—Ich weiss ein Rezept:

Schlagt in die Schallmauer Nägel.
Köpft Pusteblumen und Kerzen.
Setzt auf dem Sofa euch durch.
      Wir haben immer noch Wut.
      Schon sind wir überall heiser.
      Wir sind gegen alles umsonst.
      Was sollen wir jetzt noch machen?
      Wo sollen wir hin mit der Wut?
Mach doch was. Mach doch was.
Wir müssen irgendwas,
mach doch was, machen.
      Los, protestieren wir schnell.
      Der will nicht mitprotestieren.
      Los, unterschreib schon und schnell.
      Du warst doch immer dagegen.
      Wer nicht unterschreibt, ist dafür.
Schön ist die Wut im Gehege,
bevor sie gefüttert wird.
Lang lief die Ohnmacht im Regen,
die Strümpfe trocknet sie jetzt.
Wut und Ventile, darüber Gesang;
Ohnmacht, dein Nadelöhr ist der Gesang:
      Weil ich nichts machen kann,
      weil ich nichts machen kann,
      hab ich die Wut, hab ich die Wut.

is caressed beaten subsidized.
Already the stone that was to be moved
gathers moss, unmoved.
Can we go on like that?—Yes, in a circle.
What shall we do?—Not anything.
How express our rage?—I know a recipe:

Strike nails into the sound barrier.
Behead dandelions and candles.
Assert yourselves on the couch.
   We still feel rage.
   Already we're hoarse all over.
   We're against everything, vainly.
   What else can we do now?
   How shall we express our rage?
Do something. Do something.
We must do something or other,
do something, do it.
   Come on, then, quickly protest.
   That fellow won't join our protest.
   Come on, then, quickly sign.
   You've always been against it.
   Those who don't sign are for it.
Lovely is rage in the paddock,
before it is fed.
For a long time impotence ran around in the rain,
but now it is drying its socks.
Rage and safety valves, about them a song;
Impotence, your needle's eye is a song.
   Because I can't do anything,
   because I can't do anything
   I'm full of rage, I'm full of rage.

Mach doch was. Mach doch was.
Irgendwas. Mach doch was.
Wir müssen irgendwas,
hilft doch nix, hilft doch nix,
wir müssen irgendwas,
mach doch was, machen.
Lauf schweigend Protest.
Lief ich schon. Lief ich schon.
Schreib ein Gedicht.
Hab ich schon. Hab ich schon.
Koch eine Sülze. Schweinekopfsülze:
die Ohnmacht geliere, die Wut zittre nach.
Ich weiss ein Rezept; wer kocht es mir nach?

Do something, then. Do something.
Anything. Do something, then.
We must do something or other,
does no good, does no good,
we must do something or other,
do something, do it.
Silently march in protest.
Have done it once, have done it.
Write a poem, then.
Have written it, have done it.
Cook some brawn. Pig's head brawn:
let impotence jell, rage quiver in sympathy.
I know a recipe; who'll follow it cooking?

Die Schweinekopfsülze

Man nehme: einen halben Schweinekopf
samt Ohr und Fettbacke,
lasse die halbierte Schnauze, den Ohransatz,
die Hirnschale und das Jochbein anhacken,
lege alles mit zwei gespaltenen Spitzbeinen,
denen zuvor die blaue Schlachthofmarkierung
entfernt werden sollte,
mit nelkengespickter Zwiebel, grossem Lorbeerblatt,
mit einer Kinderhand Senfkörner
und einem gestrichenen Suppenlöffel mittlere Wut
in kochendes Salzwasser,
wobei darauf zu achten ist,
dass in geräumigem Topf alle Teile
knapp mit Wasser bedeckt sind,
und der Ohrlappen, weil er sonst ansetzt,
nicht flach auf den Topfboden gedrückt wird.
Fünf viertel Stunden lasse man kochen,
wobei es ratsam ist, nach dem ersten Aufkochen
mit der Schaumkelle
die sämigen, braungrauen Absonderungen
der inneren Schnauzenteile, sowie der Ohrmuschel
und der halbierten leeren Hirnschale
abzuschöpfen, damit wir zu einer klaren,
wenn auch geschmacksärmeren Sülze kommen,
zumal sich die rasch zum Protest gerinnende Wut,
wie jede ohnmächtige, also eiweisshaltige Leidenschaft,
wenn sie nicht rasch gleichmässig unterrührt wird,
gern in weissen Partikeln dem Schaum mitteilt.
Inzwischen wiege man vier Zwiebeln
und zwei geschälte
und vom Gehäuse befreite Äpfel
möglichst klein,

The Jellied Pig's Head

Take half a pig's head
including ear and cheek,
have the halved snout, the root of the ear,
the brainpan and the cheekbone chined,
together with two split trotters
from which the blue inspection stamp
should first have been removed,
with a clove-studded onion, a large bay leaf,
with a child's handful of mustard seed
and a level tablespoon of medium rage
place them all in boiling salt water,
taking care
that in the large pot every part
is barely covered with water
and the flap of the ear, which otherwise would stick,
is not pressed down flat on to the bottom.
  Boil gently for an hour and a quarter,
  remembering that after the first boiling-up
  it is advisable to scoop off with a ladle
  the frothy brownish-grey excretions
  from the inner part of the snout, the conch of the ear
  and the halved, empty brainpan,
  so as to obtain a pure
  though not very savoury brawn,
  particularly as the rage, which so easily curdles to protest,
  tends to communicate in white particles with the froth
  unless constantly stirred from the start.
Meanwhile chop up four onions
and two peeled
and cored apples,
preferably small,

schneide zwei Salzgurken,—
niemals Dill-, Senf- oder Delikatessgurken,—
zu winzigen Würfeln,
zerstosse in Gedanken wie im Mörser
eine gefüllte Schlüsselbeinkuhle schwarzen Pfeffer
und lasse die restliche Wut
mit beigelegter Ingwerwurzel
und wenig geriebener Zitronenschale
auf kleiner Flamme ohnmächtig ziehen.
   Sobald,—nach einer Stichprobe in die Fettbacke,—
das Kopffleisch weich ist,
die Backenzähne im Zahnbett gelockert sind,
aber noch haften,
und sich die besonders geleespendenden Hautteile
vom Ohr und an den Spalträndern
der beigelegten Spitzbeine zu lösen beginnen,
nehme man alle Teile,
sowie die nelkengespickte Zwiebel
und das Lorbeerblatt aus dem Topf,
suche mit der Schaumkelle den Topfboden
nach Knochensplittern
und den sich leicht lösenden Vorderzähnen,
sowie nach dem kiesig knirschenden Sand
der Ohrmuschel ab und lasse, während der Sud
auf kleingestelltem Feuer weiterziehen sollte,
alles auf einer Platte,
möglichst bei offenem Küchenfenster
und verengten Pupillen, abkühlen.
Jetzt gilt es, die Weichteile der Schnauze,
die Fettbacke samt eingebettetem Auge
und das darunter gelagerte Fleisch
von den Knochen zu lösen.

cut up two salted gherkins,—
never dill, mustard or vinegar pickled gherkins,—
into tiny cubes,
pound in your mind as though in a mortar
a heaped collarbone pit of black pepper
and, adding a ginger root,
as well as a little grated lemon peel,
leave the remaining rage
to simmer impotently over a low flame.
   As soon as,—after a trial jab at the cheek,—
   the meat of the head is tender,
   the back teeth are loose in the gums
   but still rooted,
   and the most jelly-conducive parts of the skin
   around the ear and the split edges
   of the added trotters begin to peel off,
   take all the components
   as well as the clove-studded onion
   and the bay leaf out of the pot,
   search the bottom with your ladle
   for bone splinters
   and the easily loosening front teeth,
   also for the grit-like grinding sand
   of the ear conch, and leave it all to cool
   on a platter,
   preferably with the kitchen windows open
   and the pupils of your eyes contracted,
   while the broth should be left to simmer
   over a low flame.
Now proceed to detach
the soft parts of the snout,
the cheek, including the eye embedded in it,
and the layers of flesh beneath them,
from the bones.

Es sei angeraten, auf weiche
bis schnittfeste Knorpelteile,
sowie auf den gallertartigen Ohrbelag,
der sich mit dem Messerrücken leichthin
vom eigentlichen Ohrlappen schaben lässt,
nicht zu verzichten,
weil gerade diese Teile,
desgleichen das lamellenförmige Zahnfleisch
und der hornige,
zur Speise- und Luftröhre leitende Zungenansatz,
unserer Sülze den speziellen
und leidenschaftlichen Sülzgeschmack geben.
Auch scheue man sich nicht,
die während der Arbeit immer wieder rasch
von einem Geleefilm überzogenen Hände
über dem dampfenden Sud abtropfen zu lassen,
weil so der Prozess des natürlichen Gelierens
abermals unterstützt wird;
denn unsere Schweinekopfsülze
soll ganz aus sich und mitgeteilter Wut,
also ohne Macht und Gelantinepapier steif werden.
Alsdann würfle man das
von den Knochen gelöste Fett und Fleisch,
desgleichen die Knorpel und Weichteile,
lege sie mit den gewiegten Zwiebeln und Äpfeln,
den winziggewürfelten Gurken,
dem gestossenen Schwarzpfeffer
und einem satten Griff Kapern in den Sud.
Mit,—nach Geschmack,—
löffelweis unterrührtem Estragonessig,—
es wird empfohlen, kräftig zu säuern,
weil Essig kalt gerne nachgibt,—

We recommend that you do not
leave out the soft
and firmer gristle
or the jelly-like covering of the ear
that can easily be scraped off with the back of a knife
from the ear flap proper,
since those very parts,
like the lamellated gums
and the horny
root of the tongue that leads to windpipe and oesophagus
impart to our brawn
that special and passionate brawn flavour.
Also, you should not fail
to let your hands, which during your work
have been covered again and again
with a film of jelly, drip dry
over the steaming broth,
because in that way the process of natural jelling
is aided once more;
for our jellied pig's head is to set
all by itself and communicated rage,
that is, without power and gelatine paper.
    Then cut up the fat and meat
    detached from the bones, not omitting the gristle,
    and together with the chopped onions and apples,
    the minutely cubed gherkins,
    the pounded black pepper,
    and an ample pinch of caper, place them in the broth.
Together with tarragon vinegar,
stirred in by the spoonful, according to taste—
we recommend a not too sparing use
because vinegar tends to weaken when cold—

lasse man alles noch einmal aufkochen,
gebe jetzt erst,
nach wenig Bedenken,
die mittlerweile
auf kleiner Flamme
schön eingedickte Wut
ohne die ausgelaugte Ingwerwurzel bei
und fülle alsdann eine zuvor
mit kaltem Wasser geschwenkte Steingutschüssel.
Diese stelle man an einen kühlen,
wenn möglich zugigen Ort
und lade sich für den nächsten Abend
freundliche Gäste ins Haus,
die eine hausgemachte Schweinekopfsülze
zu schätzen wissen.
Sparsamer Nachsatz: Wer ungern etwas verkommen lässt,
der lasse Grossknorpel und Knochen,
sowie die gespaltenen Spitzbeine
noch einmal auskochen,
verfeinere mit Majoran, Mohrrüben, Sellerie,
gebe, falls immer noch restliche Wut im Hause,
eine Messerspitze dazu
und gewinne so eine schmackhafte Suppe,
die, wenn man Wruken, Graupen, sonstige Kümmernisse
oder geschälte Erbsen beilegt,
kinderreichen Familien ein zwar einfaches,
aber nahrhaftes Essen zu ersetzen vermag.

bring it all to the boil once more,
only now, after brief hesitation,
adding the rage
which meanwhile
has well thickened
over a low flame,
without the drained ginger root,
and then proceed to fill
a stoneware dish previously rinsed with cold water.
   Place this in a cool,
   if possible draughty place
   and for the next night
   invite well-disposed guests
   who will appreciate
   a home-made pig's head brawn.
Thrifty postscriptum: people who don't like waste
should cook the coarse gristle and bones
as well as the split trotters
once again, for spice
adding marjoram, celery, carrots
and, provided more rage remains in the house,
a knife-tip of that,
so gaining a tasty soup
which, with turnips, barley, similar miseries
or dried peas
can replace for families with many children
a simple but nutritious meal.

Der Epilog

Schon hat gerechter Zorn seinen Schneider gefunden.
Sonntag glättet alltäglichen Ärger.
Ach, mit der Suppe, ohnmächtig, verkochte die Wut.
Erschöpft und gezähmt sitzen wir sanft um den Tisch.
Kleine Gewinne erfreuen den Vater; Sorge will kürzen,
denn abgestimmt, Punkt für Punkt, wird unser Haushalt.
So lässt uns Fallsucht in Ohnmacht fallen.
Immer noch werden Proteste zur Kenntnis genommen
und,—auf Verlangen,—im Protokoll erwähnt.
Es liegt ein Antrag auf Unterlassung vor:
Nie mehr soll ohne Macht protestiert werden.
Stimmlos, weil nicht beschlussfähig,
vertagen wir uns auf morgen.

The Epilogue

Already righteous indignation has found its tailor.
Sunday irons out the everyday annoyance.
Oh, with the soup, impotent rage went up in steam.
   Exhausted and tamed we gently sit round the table.
   Little gains delight Father; worries keep us short,
   for in our household point after point is put to the vote.
So falling sickness makes us fall into impotence.
Still protests are taken into consideration
and—on demand—are mentioned in the minutes.
   There is a motion for a restraining clause:
   Never again shall we protest without power.
Voiceless, because unable to constitute a quorum,
we adjourn until tomorrow.

Neue Mystik

oder: Ein kleiner Ausblick auf die utopischen Verhältnisse nach der vorläufig allerletzten Kulturrevolution.

Als unsere Fragebögen lückenhaft blieben
und die formierten Mächte sich ratlos näher kamen,
begann die Verschmelzung aller Systeme mit der Telepathie.

Während noch Skeptiker abseits standen,
wurden schon volkseigne Tische gerückt,
Geister gerufen, mit Hegel
und anderen Mystikern gefüttert,
bis es klopfte und leserlich Antwort gab.

Auf jener Tagung spiritistischer Leninisten in Lourdes,
deren Arbeitsgruppen das fortschrittliche Tibet
und die Errungenschaften der Therese von Konnersreuth
mit Hilfe der Schrenck-Notzing-Methode behandelten,
wurden die Vertreter aufklärender Dekadenz gemassregelt:
Fortan fiel Pfingsten auf jeweils den 1. Mai.

Im folgenden Jahr,
während der telepathischen Karwoche,
überführten Zen-Pioniere,
geleitet von den vierdimensionalen Sozial-Jesuiten,
gefolgt von indischen Kühen
und den grossen Sensitiven astraler Hindu-Kombinate,
des Stalin wächserne Leiche in Etappen nach Rom.

New Mysticism

or: A little survey of the utopian conditions
after the temporarily ultimate cultural revolution

When our questionnaires tended to show gaps
and the established powers, puzzled, sensed a rapprochement,
all the systems began to be merged with telepathy.

While sceptics still stood aloof,
nationalized tables were turned,
spirits invoked, then fed
on Hegel and other mystics,
until there were knocks and legible answers.

At that assembly of spiritualist Leninists at Lourdes
whose working parties dealt with progressive Tibet
and the achievements of Teresa of Konnersreuth
with the aid of the Schrenck-Notzing method,
the spokesmen for enlightened decadence were called to order:
Henceforth Whitsun always fell on the first of May.

In the following year,
during the telepathic Passion Week,
Zen pioneers,
guided by the four-dimensional Socialist Jesuits
and followed by Indian cows
as well as the great sensitives of astral Hindu Corporations
transported Stalin's wax corpse by stages to Rome.

Als man, nach paladinischer Weisung,
(Eusapia Paladino, geb. 1854 in Neapel,
mediale Vorkämpferin der Neuen Mystik)
auf der windigen Insel Gotland
ein gelbhaariges Medium gefunden hatte,
wurde es zur Heldin des sozialistischen Mystizismus erklärt
und kurz nach jenem tragischen Autounfall,—
versprengte Sozialdemokraten
und marxistische Revisionisten
gestanden später den Anschlag,—
heiliggesprochen.

Die in Texas und in der Äusseren Mongolei
zwecks Umschulung an Schutzlagertischen
konzentrierten Konterrevolutionäre
nehmen fortan
von Sitzung zu Sitzung ab.

Ständig tagt unser Vollzirkel dialektischer Psychokinese.
Denn immer noch gibt die Heilige Antwort.
Um einen Tisch sitzt die Welt und holt Rat bei ihr.
Sie, die irrationale, rüstet uns ab,
sie, die telekinetische, hilft uns, das Soll zu erfüllen,
sie, die okkulte, ernährt und verwaltet uns,
nur sie, die parteiliche und unfehlbare,
sie, die gebenedeite und schmerzensreiche,
sie, die liebliche Sensitive,
füllt unsere Fragebögen,
benennt unsere Strassen,
säubert uns gründlich,
erlöst uns vom Zweifel,
nimmt uns das Kopfweh.

When, in accordance with paladinian instructions
(Eusapia Paladino, born 1854 in Naples,
medium and forerunner of the New Mysticism)
on the windy Isle of Jutland
a yellow-haired medium had been found,
she was proclaimed heroine of socialist mysticism
and shortly after that tragic motor accident,—
scattered Social Democrats
and Marxist revisionists
later confessed to the coup,—
she was canonized.

The counter-revolutionaries
concentrated in Texas and Outer Mongolia
for the purpose of re-education at the desks of protective camps
now diminish
from meeting to meeting.

Our plenary circle of dialectical psychokinesis is in permanent
session.
For still the saint answers questions.
Around one table the world sits and asks for advice.
She, the irrational, disarms us,
she, the telekinetic, helps us to fulfil the norm,
she, the occult, feeds and administers us,
only she, the partisan and infallible,
she, the blessed and sorrowful,
she, the charmingly sensitive,
fills in our questionnaires,
gives names to our streets,
cleanses us thoroughly,
delivers us from doubts,
takes away our headache.

Fortan müssen wir nicht mehr denken,
nur noch gehorchen
und ihre Klopfzeichen auswerten.

From now on we need no longer think,
only obey
and decode her knocking signals.

Kleckerburg

Gestrichnes Korn, gezielte Fragen
verlangt die Kimme lebenslang:
Als ich verliess den Zeugenstand,
an Wände, vor Gericht gestellt,
wo Grenzen Flüsse widerlegen,
sechstausend Meter überm Mief,
zuhause, der Friseur behauchte
den Spiegel und sein Finger schrieb:
Geboren wann? Nun sag schon, wo?
Das liegt nordöstlich, westlich von
und nährt noch immer Fotografen.
Das hiess mal so, heut heisst es so.
Dort wohnten bis, von dann an wohnten.
Ich buchstabiere: Wrzeszcz hiess früher.
Das Haus blieb stehen, nur der Putz.
Den Friedhof, den ich, gibts nicht mehr.
Wo damals Zäune, kann heut jeder.
So gotisch denkt sich Gott was aus.
Denn man hat wieder für viel Geld.
Ich zählte Giebel, keiner fehlte:
das Mittelalter holt sich ein.
Nur jenes Denkmal mit dem Schwanz
ist westwärts und davon geritten.
Und jedes Pausenzeichen fragt;
denn als ich, zwischen Muscheln, kleckerte mit Sand,
als ich bei Brenntau einen Grabstein fand,
als ich Papier bewegte im Archiv
und im Hotel die Frage in fünf Sprachen:
Geboren wann und wo, warum?
nach Antwort schnappte, beichtete mein Stift:
     Das war zur Zeit der Rentenmark.
     Hier, nah der Mottlau, die ein Nebenfluss,

Kleckerburg

Aimed questions, foresight well aligned
lifelong the backsight will demand:
When I had left the witness box,
stood up in court, before a wall,
where frontiers contravert the rivers,
twelve thousand feet above the smog,
at home, the barber breathed upon
his mirror, and his finger wrote:
Born when? And—out with it—born where?
   It lies to the north-east, west of,
   and still can feed photographers.
   Its name was this and now is that.
   There lived until, from then on lived.
   I spell: its name was Wrzeszcz before.
   The house still stands, but the façade.
   The graveyard, which, has ceased to be.
   Where fences were now anyone.
   Such gothic things does God think up.
   For once again at great expense.
   I counted gables, none was missing:
   The Middle Ages catch us up.
   Only that statue with the tail
   has ridden off now, has gone west.
And every station signal also asks;
for when, between small shells, I built sand castles,
when I unearthed a tombstone outside Brenntau,
when I turned over papers in the archives
and in five languages the form in the hotel:
Born when and where, block letters please, born why?
yapped for the answers, my ball pen confessed:
   It was when *Rentenmarks* were current.
   Here, by the Mottlau, a small tributary,

wo Forster brüllte und Hirsch Fajngold schwieg,
hier, wo ich meine ersten Schuhe
zerlief, und als ich sprechen konnte,
das Stottern lernte: Sand, klatschnass,
zum Kleckern, bis mein Kinder-Gral
sich gotisch türmte und zerfiel.

Das war knapp zwanzig Jahre nach Verdun;
und dreissig Jahre Frist, bis mich die Söhne
zum Vater machten; Stallgeruch
hat diese Sprache, Sammeltrieb,
als ich Geschichten, Schmetterlinge spiesste
und Worte fischte, die gleich Katzen
auf Treibholz zitterten, an Land gesetzt,
zwölf Junge warfen: grau und blind.

Geboren wann? Und wo? Warum?
Das hab ich hin und her geschleppt,
im Rhein versenkt, bei Hildesheim begraben;
doch Taucher fanden und mit Förderkörben
kam Strandgut Rollgut hoch, ans Licht.

Bucheckern, Bernstein, Brausepulver,
dies Taschenmesser und dies Abziehbild,
ein Stück vom Stück, Tonnagezahlen,
Minutenzeiger, Knöpfe, Münzen,
für jeden Platz ein Tütchen Wind.

Hochstapeln lehrt mein Fundbüro:
Gerüche, abgetretne Schwellen,
verjährte Schulden, Batterien,
die nur in Taschenlampen glücklich,
und Namen, die nur Namen sind:
Elfriede Broschke, Siemoneit,
Guschnerus, Lusch und Heinz Stanowski;
auch Chodowiecki, Schopenhauer
sind dort geboren. Wann? Warum?

where Forster roared, Hirsch Fajngold held his tongue,
where I wore out the soles of my first pair
of shoes, and being old enough to speak
learned how to stammer: sand, all clammy
for making castles, until my childhood grail
gothically towered and collapsed.
That was some twenty years after Verdun;
came thirty years of respite, till my sons
made me a father; stable smells
talk in this lilt, collector's mania
when stories, butterflies I impaled
and fished for words that cat-like trembled
on rafts of driftwood washed ashore,
gave birth to twelve, all grey and blind.
Born when? And where? Block letters please. And why?
Those questions I have dragged around,
sunk in the Rhine, buried near Hildesheim;
but divers found them and in dragging nets
flotsam and jetsam rose, were brought to light.
Beechnuts and amber, sherbet fizz,
this pen-knife and this transfer picture,
piece of a piece, ship tonnage figures,
buttons and coins and minute hands,
for every square a bag of wind.
To confidence tricks I'm driven by
my treasure trove, lost property office:
The smells, the thresholds trodden down,
debts never paid, small batteries
happy in torches, only torches,
and names that are no more than names:
Elfriede Broschke, Siemoneit,
Guschnerus, Lusch and Heinz Stanowski;
and Chodowiecki, Schopenhauer
were born there too. Born when? Born why?

Ja, in Geschichte war ich immer gut.
Fragt mich nach Pest und Teuerung.
Ich bete läufig Friedensschlüsse,
die Ordensmeister, Schwedennot,
und kennen alle Jagellonen
und alle Kirchen, von Johann
bis Trinitatis, backsteinrot.
Wer fragt noch wo? Mein Zungenschlag
ist baltisch tückisch stubenwarm.
Wie macht die Ostsee?—Blubb, pifff, pschsch . . .
Auf deutsch, auf polnisch: Blubb, pifff, pschsch . . .
Doch als ich auf dem volksfestmüden,
von Sonderbussen, Bundesbahn
gespeisten Flüchtlingstreffen in Hannover
die Funktionäre fragte, hatten sie
vergessen, wie die Ostsee macht,
und liessen den Atlantik röhren;
ich blieb beharrlich: Blubb, pifff, pschsch . . .
Da schrien alle: Schlagt ihn tot!
Er hat auf Menschenrecht und Renten,
auf Lastenausgleich, Vaterstadt
verzichtet, hört den Zungenschlag:
Das ist die Ostsee nicht, das ist Verrat.
Befragt ihn peinlich, holt den Stockturm her,
streckt, rädert, blendet, brecht und glüht,
passt dem Gedächtnis Schrauben an.
Wir wollen wissen, wo und wann.
Nicht auf Strohdeich und Bürgerwiesen,
nicht in der Pfefferstadt,—ach, wär ich doch
geboren zwischen Speichern auf dem Holm!—
in Striessbachnähe, nah dem Heeresanger
ist es passiert, heut heisst die Strasse

Yes, I was always good at history.
Ask me about the plagues and price increases.
Peace treaties fluently I can pray,
masters of orders, Swedish war,
and all the Jagellons I know,
and all the churches, from St. John's
to Holy Trinity, red brick.
    Who still asks where? My intonation
is Baltic, wily, warm as rooms.
What says the Baltic? Blubb, pfff, pshsh . . .
In German, Polish: Blubb, pfff, pshsh . . .
But when I asked the functionaries
at the assembly-weary, coach-
and-special-train-fed gathering
of eastern refugees at Hanover,
they had forgotten what the Baltic says
and made the Atlantic Ocean roar;
I kept insisting: Blubb, pfff, pshsh . . .
So: Hit him! Kill him! all yelled out,
he's turned his back on human rights,
on pensions, on his native city,
on compensations, restitutions,
just listen to his intonation:
That's not the Baltic, that's high treason.
Put screws on him and make him talk,
get wheels and tongs and pokers, blind him,
and stretch his memory on the rack.
    We want his answer: when and where.
Not on the Straw Dyke, nor in Merchants' Meadows,
nor yet in Pepper Town—would that I had
been born between great store lofts on the Holm!—
Near the small Striessbach, by the Rifle Range
it happened, and today the street

auf polnisch Lelewela,—nur die Nummer
links von der Haustür blieb und blieb.
Und Sand, klatschnass, zum Kleckern: Gral . . .
In Kleckerburg gebürtig, westlich von.
Das liegt nordwestlich, südlich von.
Dort wechselt Licht viel schneller als.
Die Möwen sind nicht Möwen, sondern.
Und auch die Milch, ein Nebenarm der Weichsel,
floss mit dem Honig brückenreich vorbei.
Getauft geimpft gefirmt geschult.
Gespielt hab ich mit Bombensplittern.
Und aufgewachsen bin ich zwischen
dem Heilgen Geist und Hitlers Bild.
Im Ohr verblieben Schiffssirenen,
gekappte Sätze, Schreie gegen Wind,
paar heile Glocken, Mündungsfeuer
und etwas Ostsee: Blubb, pifff, pschsch . . .

in Polish is called Lelewela—only
the number left of the door remains, remains.
And sand, for castles, clammy, muddy: grail . . .
At Kleckerburg was born, west of.
It lies to the northwest, south of.
The light there changes much more than.
The seagulls are not seagulls, but.
And there the Milch, a Vistula tributary,
honeyed and many-bridged flowed by.
    Baptized and vaccinated, schooled, confirmed.
    Bomb splinters, meanwhile, were my toys.
    And I grew up, was reared between
    the Holy Ghost and Hitler's photograph.
    Ships' sirens echo in my ears,
    lopped sentences and wind-blown cries,
    a few sound churchbells, rifle fire
    and Baltic snatches: Blubb, pfff, pshsh . . .

Sechsundsechzig

In diesem Eidechsenjahr,—
wirklich, auf sonnigem Putz
atmeten viele verspielt . . .

In diesem Jahr unterwegs,—
was mich beschleunigt, wächst,
gibt Zeichen, hat überholt . . .

In diesem Jahr kinderleicht,—
Jahr, das befürchten lässt: Schrott . . .

In diesem kosmischen Jahr,—
fortschreitend witzlos verläuft . . .

In diesem Jahr auf ein Jahr,—
Jahr ohne Gag Richtung Mond . . .

In diesem Bilderschirmjahr,—
Eckbälle wurden verschossen,
Schreckschüsse sassen im Tor . . .

Im sechsundsechzigsten Jahr
tobte im Kies, zu Füssen der Mauer:
ein unwiderrufner Befehl,
bewegter Protest,
ledige Wut:
zwei Eidechsenschwänze.

Sixty-six

In this lizard year,—
   really, on sunny plaster
     many playfully breathed . . .

In this year on my way,—
   what accelerates me, grows,
     gives me signals, has overtaken . . .

In this year childishly simple,—
   year that portends: scrap . . .

In this cosmic year,—
   progressively witlessly passes . . .

In this year for a year,—
   year without gag direction moon . . .

In this television screen year,—
   corner shots went foul,
     alarm shots struck the goal . . .

In the year sixty-six
   raged in the gravel, at the foot of the Wall:
     an order not rescinded,
       lively protest,
         sheer rage:
           two lizard tails.

Luft holen

Seife und Äpfel kaufen.
Möwen habe ich schon beschrieben.
Diese sind kleiner.

Eisgrütze auf den Grachten igelt sich ein.
Wer hat die Mädchen
mit Graupeln beworfen: zu fettes Essen?

Man sagt, die Königin subventioniere
die Fahrräder.
Und eine der Tulpen heisst: Lustige Witwe.

Es ist schon so, dass die Zwiebel,
wenn man sie streichelt,
am Ende ja sagt.

Tagsüber lache ich vor mich hin.
Das darf man hier:
vorsichhinlachen und luftholen.

Taking Breath

Buy soap and apples.
Seagulls—I've described them before.
These are smaller.

Ice scum on the canals curls up.
Who chucked sleet
at the girls: too rich food?

They say that the queen
subsidizes bicycles.
And one of the tulips is called Merry Widow.

It is established,
that when you stroke it the bulb
says yes in the end.

All day long I laugh to myself.
That's allowed here:
laughing to oneself and taking breath.

Im Botanischen Garten

Die Farbenreiber leben vom Herbst.
Fünfhundert Sorten Erica,
darunter das Kräutchen Calluna der Besenheide.
Am Sonntag Familienauftrieb:
neben Begonien und weisser Vollendung,
nahe dem Ricinus,
wächst das Vivil für den übrigen Groschen,
unseren Atem zu klären.
Nacktsamer und Farne.
Leguminosae,—unsere Liebe, Hülsenfrucht,
Scheinhasel, Zaubernuss, flüchtet sich ins Latein.—
Auf verwaschenen Schildchen
springt sie und springt
von der kanadischen Felsenbirne,
zu deren Füssen Kastanien spotten,
zum morgenländischen Lebensbaum,
der kein Laub wirft und Friedhöfen nahe steht.
  Wir lernten uns bei der blassen Miss Winett kennen.
  Im Jahre neununddreissig züchtete Otto Greul
  seine Teehybride Gretl Greul.
Wegen deiner verzweigten Verwandtschaft
stritten wir uns
unterm getüpfelten Blasenstrauch.
  Diese Rose vorm weissen Tausendschön,
  neben der kniehoch kriechenden Floribunda,
  diese Rose wurde nach einem General benannt:
Mac Arthur. Mac Arthur. Die Rose Mac Arthur.
Nichts schreckt die Kinder,
denn zwischen Anzuchten sind alle gerollten Schlangen
sonntäglich ruhende Schläuche,
montags die Pyrenäen zu wässern,
dienstags das Amurland und so weiter . . .
  Dort, unterm Judasbaum,
  Herzblätter wirft er,
  wird eine Bank frei.

In the Botanical Garden

The dye-makers live on autumn.
Five hundred varieties of heather,
among them the little herb calluna the ling.
   On Sundays family round-up:
   next to begonias and white perfection,
   near the ricinus,
   Mentha grows for the penny left over
   to purify our breath.
Gymnospera and ferns.
Leguminosae,—our love, edible seed,
false hazel, magic nut, takes refuge in Latin.—
On blurred little tabs
she jumps and jumps
from the Canadian rock pear
at whose foot chestnuts mock,
to the Eastern tree of life
that sheds no leaves, congenial to graveyards.
   We became acquainted at pale Miss Winett's.
   In 'thirty-nine Otto Greul grew
   his tea hybrid Gretl Greul.
Because of the distant relationship
we quarrelled
under the spotted bladder nut.
   This rose in front of the white daisies,
   next to the floribunda creeping knee-high,
   this rose was called after a general:
   MacArthur. MacArthur. The MacArthur rose.
Nothing frightens the children,
for between beds all the curled-up snakes
are hosepipes resting on Sundays,
Mondays to water the Pyrenees,
Tuesdays the land of Amur etc. . . .
   There, under the Judas tree,
   shedding heart-shaped leaves,
   a seat is being vacated.

Vermont

Zum Beispiel Grün. In sich zerstritten Grün.
Grün kriecht bergan, erobert seinen Markt;
so billig sind geweisste Häuser hier zu haben.

Wer sich dies ausgedacht, dem fällt
zum Beispiel immer neues Grün
in Raten ein, der wiederholt sich nie.

Geräte ruhen, grünlich überwunden,
dabei war Rost ihr rötester Beschluss,
der eisern vorlag, nun als Schrott zu haben.

Wir schlugen Feuerschneisen, doch es wuchs
das neue Grün viel schneller als
und grüner als zum Beispiel Rot.

Wenn dieses Grün erbrochen wird.
Zum Beispiel Herbst: die Wälder legen
den Kopfschmuck an und wandern aus.

Ich war mal in Vermont, dort ist es grün . . .

Vermont

For instance green. A green at odds with green.
Green creeps uphill and wins itself a market;
here houses painted white go for a song.

Whoever thought this up discovers
new green for instance in perpetual
instalments, never repeats himself.

Tools lie around, all greenly overcome
though rust had been their reddest resolution,
iron when formed, now to be bought as scrap.

We burned our way through woods, but the new green
grew far too fast, much faster than
and greener than for instance red.

When this same green is broken up.
For instance autumn: the woods put on
their head adornments and migrate.

Once I was in Vermont, there it is green . . .

Falsche Schönheit

Diese Stille,
    also der abseits in sich verbissne Verkehr,
      gefällt mir,
und dieses Hammelkotelett,
    wenn es auch kalt mittlerweile und talgig,
      schmeckt mir,
das Leben,
    ich meine die Spanne seit gestern bis Montag früh,
      macht wieder Spass:
ich lache über Teltower Rübchen,
unser Meerschweinchen erinnert mich rosa,
Heiterkeit will meinen Tisch überschwemmen,
und ein Gedanke,
    immerhin ein Gedanke,
      geht ohne Hefe auf;
        und ich freue mich,
          weil er falsch ist und schön.

Wrong Beauty

This quiet,
   that is, the traffic some way off, its teeth stuck into itself,
     pleases me,
and this lamb cutlet,
   though cold by now and greasy,
     tastes good,
life,
   I mean the period from yesterday to Monday morning,
     is fun again:
I laugh at the dish of parsnips,
our guinea pig pinkly reminds me,
cheerfulness threatens to flood my table,
and an idea,
   an idea of sorts,
     rises without yeast;
       and I'm happy
         because it is wrong and beautiful.

März

Schon wieder mischen sie Beton.
Von rostiger Armierung taut
die letzte Hemmung, Fertigteile
verfügen sich und stehen stramm:
Komm. Pass dich an. Komm. Pass dich an.
Als meine Wut den Horizont verbog,
als ich den Müll nicht schlucken wollte,
als ich mit kleinen spitzen Verben
Bereifung schlitzte,—Warum parken Sie?—
als ich den Pudding durch ein Haarsieb hetzte
und ihm sein rosa Gegenteil bewies,
als ich mir Schatten fing, als Schattenfänger
bezahlt, danach veranlagt wurde,
als ich die Nägel himmelwärts
durch frischgestrichne Bänke trieb,
als ich Papier, mit Hass bekritzelt,
zu Schiffchen faltete und schwimmen liess,
als Liebe einen Knochen warf
und meine Zunge sich Geschmack erdachte,
als ich beschloss, die Gürtelrose zu besprechen,
nur weil im Welken noch drei Gramm Genuss,
als ich, es nieselte, die Bronze leckte
und schwellenscheu die Fotzen heilig sprach,
als meine Finger läufig wurden
und längs den Buden jedes Astloch deckten,
als ich die Automaten, bis game over,
bei kleinen Stössen Klingeln lehrte,
als jede Rechnung unterm Strich
auf minus neunundsechzig zählte,
als ich bei Tauben lag und schwören musste:
Nie wieder werde ich mit Möwen!—
als ich ein Ohr besprang, um Ablass bat:

March

Again they're mixing concrete now.
From rusty armatures the last
small inhibition thaws, spare parts
stand at attention, fit for use:
Come on. Adapt. Come on. Adapt.
  When my great fury twisted the horizon,
  when I refused to swallow garbage,
  when with my little pointed verbs
  I slit the tyres,—why are you parking here?—
  when through a hair sieve I made the pudding squelch
  and gave it proof of its pink opposite,
  when I caught shadows and, remunerated,
  was taxed for it, profession: shadow-catcher,
  when heavenward I drove my nails
  through newly painted garden seats,
  when I took paper scribbled full of hate,
  folded it into boats and launched them,
  when love chucked me a bone, and then
  my tongue devised a relish for its taste,
  when I decided to cure shingles with a spell
  since even detumescence gives three grammes of pleasure,
  when—on a drizzly day—I licked the bronze
  and, shy of thresholds, canonized all cunts,
  when my ten fingers suddenly were in rut
  and served each knot-hole in that row of shacks,
  when, till game over, with little tilts and pushes
  I taught the slot machines to ring,
  when every bill beneath the line
  came out as minus nine pounds ten,
  when with the doves I lay and had to vow:
  never again I'll do it with the seagulls!—
  mounted an ear and begged for mercy, wheedling:

Zu trocken sind die Engel und zu eng!—
als nur noch Kopfstand mir Vokabeln gab:
Ich liebe dich. Ich liebe dich.—
Als Winterfutter aus den Mänteln
geknöpft und eingemottet wurde,
als sich das Treibhaus bunt erbrach,—
Lautsprecher in den März gestellt,—
als Kitzel Krätze Fisch und Lauch
sich stritten, brach der Frühling aus:
Ich hab genug. Komm. Zieh dich aus.

Too dry the angels are, too tight!—
when only headstands yielded phrases still:
I love you, dear. I love you, dear.—
When winter linings were unbuttoned
from overcoats and, moth-proofed, put away,
when garishly the greenhouse puked,—
loudspeaker blaring into March,—
when tickle scratches fish and leek
began to quarrel, spring broke out:
Come on now. Get undressed, girl. Quick.